Masterminding
YOUR SUCCESS ▲
▲

A Teaching, Learning and Exercise Manual

for Coping with Stress at School, Home and Work,

for Children, Teens and Adults.

A Comprehensive Book with Over 30 Exercises.

▶ **Henry L. Janzen,** Ph.D., Psychologist

▶ **John G. Paterson,** Ed. D., Psychologist

▶ **Carl Blashko,** M.D., F.R.C.P.(C), Psychiatrist

Printed in Canada

Canadian Cataloguing in Publication Data
Janzen, Henry

Masterminding your success: coping with stress at home, school and work.

Includes bibliographical references.
ISBN 0-9694322-2-4

1. Stress management.   I.   Paterson, John G.,
II. Blashko, Carl-   III. Title

BF575.S75J36 1993   155.9'042 C93-090140-1

Published by
Three Pears Publishing
922 Burley Drive
Edmonton, Alberta T6R 1X3

Other publications
That's Living
That's Living, Too
When You Stand Alone

TABLE OF CONTENTS

FOREWORD

The title of this book "*Masterminding Your Success*" originated from the thousands of discussions we have had with people from all walks of life. While each author is a professor, researcher and clinician, it was the nine years as co-hosts on a popular, daily radio show that gave us the desire to share our views with the public. Most listeners and callers looked upon us as warm, caring, knowledgeable hosts. We were truly humbled by this. Although we teach at the University, what we read and studied needed to be translated for the public into an intellectually honest and understandable form. College teaching forced us to do this, but not as much as the radio show. As a result we wrote two books, *That's Living* and *That's Living, Too* based on major questions asked of us over and over again on-air. We restricted the third book, *When You Stand Alone* to one question, namely, how to cope with loneliness. This book, our fourth written for the general public, summarizes key stress management techniques in four primary settings: the workplace, the home, the marriage, and the school. The responsibility is ours. Nothing will happen unless we "take the bull by the horns."

Hank Janzen
John Paterson
Carl Blashko

INTRODUCTION

Masterminding Your Success is a practical book about how to survive the stressors at home, at work, at school and in the family. It is much more than a stress management guide. It is our philosophy of living, nurtured by years of study, research, lecturing and dealing with public questions on radio, television and print. The authors are professionals in the health and education sector of society. We believe as strongly in prevention as we do in treatment. Our experiences can be summarized in one small poem:

> *To all my faults my eyes are blind.*
> *Mine are the sins I cannot find.*
> *But your mistakes I see aplenty.*
> *For them my eyes are 20/20.*
> *- H.L.J.*

People have an automatic impulse to protect themselves in times of danger. They attack or they hide. Either way, the natural tendency is to ignore or avoid focusing on one's weaknesses. To do so is to invite defeat. So we hide from ourselves and attack others so that our vulnerabilities won't show. Sometimes this works and so it reinforces the strategy. Next time we are under attack, we'll try it again.

What this book does is force us to build up our own resources so as to welcome inner reflection. It focuses on what we can all do to become winners instead of victims. There is a great tendency in our society to blame others for our problems and then bitterly complain that we are victims. This book will help you put the responsibility for success squarely on your own shoulders.

We do this deliberately, not to frighten, but to encourage. You see, we believe in people. We believe in the worth of every single human being. We believe in our power to change. We believe that people have more resources than are used. The trick is to get you to believe it too. If you believe in yourself, then the process of growth can begin.

Thus, the book begins with the concept of stress, its meaning and its effect,moves to stress coping skills for personal use, then on to the workplace, the school, the home and the marriage. Since most homes have both partners in the workplace, we devote a chapter to balancing home and work. The book is replete with practical suggestions in every chapter. We could have given you the research sources for most of the techniques, but we chose, instead, to give you the sources at the back of the book. There is one unusual chapter on fantasy development in the child. This was written to emphasize the inner power of the person as a natural development from birth to adulthood. Fantasy, when used in moderation, is a powerful healing technique. We end with a potpourri of ideas on practical, everyday concerns.

We hope you enjoy this short book. It is a compilation of techniques and strategies that we have used with our own patients and taught at numerous workshops for businesses, hospitals, schools, and parent-groups. The book will add information to what can be said in a lecture or demonstration. It can be used as your guide to success!

EXERCISES

Chapter One

THE MEANING OF STRESS

Introduction

Medical doctors tell us that stress is the cause of many of our emotional and physical illnesses. They caution that it would be wise not to wait for science to ascertain the link between stress and these illnesses, but rather, to do something about it now! Perhaps we should adopt what the Chinese called the "Moi Sui" wisdom and stop using technical doubts as an excuse for not tackling the problem until it's too late. Let the scientists weigh factors like diet, heredity and environment, but in the meantime assume that failure to cope with stress is a major contributing factor in heart attacks, hypertension, angina, arrhythmia, migraines, peptic ulcers, colitis, diabetes, gastro-intestinal disorders, low back pain and possibly even cancer. Stress is known to lower our resistance to all kinds of infectious diseases such as colds and influenza. Stress slows down recovery and therefore make us more liable for continued physical as well as emotional illnesses. The effect of stress worsens our mental state. Once we face more stress than we can handle, we get the physical illnesses which further complicate our lives. While we are under stress we tend to poison the atmosphere emotionally, thus making other people's lives miserable. Stress is also known to cause careless accidents because under stress we lose concentration as well as efficiency and effectiveness.

It is important for us to start thinking about this because our reaction to stress can affect everything we do. Perhaps it is useful, right at the outset, to state our very own definition of stress. We feel that stress is a physical, mental and emotional reaction to events or thoughts. Stress is not "out there." Stress is a reaction to our inner perceptions of what is out there. For example, one driver may be relaxed in traffic while another may be upset, impatient, angry and hostile. The first driver simply accepts the traffic and the other drivers. The second driver may be perceiving other drivers as "bad" or "idiots" and therefore reacts to them as if they are "bad." In other words, it is not the drivers that give us stress, but what we think of those drivers.

As you can see, each person has a unique way of dealing with stress. What affects one person may not affect another in the same way. Stress is usually seen in a negative light since adverse reactions are possible. However, positive events can cause the same physical and emotional reaction in the body. It is only when we repeatedly experience unpleasant thoughts and feelings that we give it the label "stress." Thus, stress is technically seen as anything that arouses the physical, mental and emotional systems in people, that over time causes serious problems at home, work and in the body. There are many other technical definitions that may vary from ours but we feel that this definition is an adequate and practical explanation of what we mean by stress. Many people use the word "burnout" and stress synonymously. We see burnout as a reaction to stress, and not the stress itself. Burnout could be considered a final stage of stress in which people are negatively affected in body and mind thus lowering their productivity. When we discuss the stages of stress you will see that burnout happens to be a distinct phase of the stress response.

The Super Well Person

It is often useful to have some criteria by which we can measure what is wrong with us by knowing what is right with us. We now want to look at some indicators of what being well means. If we fall short in these areas we know that we must be not well, or experiencing stress. To do this, we have devised a symptom checklist of criteria which defines the super well person. Have a look at this list and see how many of them apply to you.

THE SUPER WELL PERSON

☆ Deeply committed to an altruistic cause
☆ Seldom sick
☆ Others lean on you in crisis
☆ Comfortable with the spiritual side of life
☆ Clear sense of purpose at home and at work
☆ Sharp, curious mind, sense of humor
☆ Well-organized - gets lots done
☆ Able to live and enjoy the present
☆ Do not look back or to the future all the time
☆ Comfortable with a wide range of emotions
☆ Accepting one's limitations, mistakes and handicaps
☆ Able and willing to take charge of one's life
☆ Practices positive self-care and assertiveness
☆ Feels good to be alive

The super well person experiences the ups and downs of life like all others, but comes to grips with them quicker. All of us will experience a major setback and loss from time to time. Some get over it and others do not, at least not as quickly. The super well person is able to overcome these crises. People have asked us how long it should take for someone to get over the death of a loved one, for example. There is no easy answer to this because people are very different in how they respond to such a great crisis. The super well person may need treatment but will get over the loss within six months to two years and then get on with life with a new sense of direction and purpose. While the loss is never forgotten, the person can still laugh and smile in the face of the setbacks that have been experienced. The super well person can be depressed but has also found a way to overcome that illness. The super well person will get angry or can find ways to turn anger into joy. Keep in mind that we all feel super well from time to time. The test of our health, however, is that we are able to bounce back more quickly than others if we are healthy in spirit, mind and body.

Understanding the Stress Reaction

Dr. Peter Hanson, in his book *Joy of Stress*, argues that as a casino exists simply by stacking the odds in its favour, so must we, in our daily lives, stack the decks in our favour. Many of the so-called stressors in our life need not exist. Sometimes we simply choose a life style or a goal in which our wants exceed our means. For instance, think of those purchases (wants) that put us into debt--and stress. Such a life style in and out of itself will cause physical and emotional reactions, reactions that we know as stress. Of course, many experiences in life are not self-induced, such as the death of a loved one, a motor vehicle accident, unemployment, nuclear threat, rejection by peers or a traumatic break-up with a friend. Being an outstanding student or a student that is failing an exam may not be a self-induced cause of stress. So stress can come to us from any direction but by and large how we think and deal with it inside is what is important. Let us look at some examples of arousal. If you are daydreaming and very relaxed, the ringing of the door bell may "arouse" you. You are more alert and awake. When we are at a movie, however, we may get extremely aroused when we watch a death scene. And we may become sexually aroused if we view a seduction scene in a movie, but if the movie is boring our arousal is reduced and we fall asleep.

Hans Selye is a physician and endocrinologist. He has written more than 30 books and 600 scientific papers. He is a man that has been awarded sixteen honourary degrees and could lecture in ten languages. This man has written about stress more than any other we know. Selye said that we still may not know properly how to cope with stress, but we do know how the body reacts to it. He defined stress in two ways. First, there is a **specific reaction**. This is a very special kind of reaction to a special kind of stress. For example, if you are riding in a car and somebody suddenly crosses your path, your body will immediately react and you may experience an intense surge in the pit of your stomach. This is a specific reaction to a specific event. The same thing can happen when somebody suddenly calls your name. Your mind has responded and immediately there is an intense feeling inside. Selye identified a second reaction called a **non-specific reaction** to stress. This reaction is the same in terms of the body physiology no matter what stress we experience. The nervous system reacts to all stimuli that impact on its sensory mechanisms in the same way. In other words, while specific reactions differ, the non-specific ones never do. This means that whether something is positive or negative, unpleasant or joyful, physical or mental, the non-specific reaction is always the same. We can explain it this way. We know that receiving a kiss is not the same as taking poison. Yet both are stressors. They have different specific results and they also have non-specific results. The specific reaction to a kiss would be heightened arousal and much emotional pleasure. The specific reaction to poison would be heightened arousal and anxiety and a mental and emotional depression associated with the partaking of the poison. In terms of the non-specific results, the body would react in the same way emotionally and mentally to these two events. On both occasions our heart rate, blood pressure, breathing rate and perspiration rate would increase. It is only the mind that interprets them differently.

Selye also said that, by and large, we have many ways of dealing with specific reactions to stress but only two ways of dealing with non-specific reactions. You see, in specific reactions and special circumstances we can respond very differently. If we are offered a kiss we might be quite aroused. If we are threatened we might get very angry. These are very different reactions. However, when our body reacts in a non-specific way it usually does so in two ways. First, by fighting it. This is called a **catatoxic reaction**. Secondly, by adapting to the stress. This is called a **syntoxic reaction**. So in the end, when the stressors of life pile up, we really only have two ways of coping with stress.

The other thing to keep in mind is that when stress builds up, our body, through the influence of the mind, begins to react in a non-specific way to most everything that happens to us. When this is the case, the result can be quite disastrous in terms of one's physical, mental and emotional health. Throughout this book we will mention specific as well as non-specific ways of coping with stress. We will show that if the body repeatedly reacts in the same way to different situations, stress is building up to the point where the individual can no longer cope with it effectively. We will present exercises that will help you come to grips with your specific stress reaction and the possible causes. Changes in life style may be necessary or stress management techniques may have to be learned in order to become, once again, the super well person.

Stress As An Individual Matter

We see stress as highly individual. It is related to how you look at a situation, appraise it as threatening or pleasant, and then react to it in some way. Think of how you would take a snapshot. You scan the scene and focus your camera, you decide what aspect to snap into the picture frame, and then the picture is reduced from three dimensions to two and you take the picture. You can see right now that the consequence of this is that a lot of information is sacrificed. The larger picture, the other things outside the picture are simply not taken in. In this analogy the settings make all the difference. For example, lens quality and type would make a difference in terms of determining what kind of picture you would get. Focus and clarity as well as detail and depth would make a big difference as to the kind of picture you take. Just think of how many filters you can put on your camera to change the nature of the picture. Speed-setting is also very important. The amount of light you let in will be affected by whether the object is standing still or whether you are taking a picture of a moving vehicle.

Most of the reactions to your life are determined psychologically in this very same manner. Your self-confidence, your upbringing, your values and attitudes, the quality of your inner resources and your existing thinking-style all determine how well you cope and what pictures you take in life. Essentially, the first shot you take evaluates the nature of the situation and whether it is likely to be pleasant, neutral or noxious. In other words, situations may be seen as 'good', 'bad' or 'indifferent.' The first picture is usually based on pre-existing beliefs, attitudes or expectations. This picture is the most important because it determines the next reactions and the next view of the situation. The first picture calls for your critical response. You have a choice of making an emergency response or a confidence response. An emergency response may be blocking the picture from one's mind or depreciating it. A confidence response may be in smiling or in feeling confident about what you have seen and what picture you have taken. The first shot also evaluates not only the risk but your resources to cope. If you feel you don't have the resources, the perceived stress will increase and thus be very high. First picture responses are automatic. They refer to Selye's 'fight' or 'flight' reaction. We do not deliberate, compute and evaluate. Our reactions are highly subjective, fast and impulsive. So when we react to something, we do it on our first shot and many times our first shot is an exaggerated response to a situation.

We would also like to focus on areas of attitudes and values as they impact on stress. This is a very important matter because attitudes and values largely determine how we react to our family, our children, our home and our work. An attitude is a more or less stable set of opinions, interests or purposes, involving expectancies of a certain kind of experience and a readiness with a certain kind of appropriate response. A value, on the other hand, is a standard or unit. Values refer to worth, merit or importance. Usually values are any things or ideas considered desirable that we regard or esteem highly. So values have a dimension, a name, and a magnitude. That is we estimate them at a certain personal level and they have importance. Values can be very important or not so important. Values can be positive or negative, subjective or objective.

The differentiation between attitudes and values is quite important. While attitudes are usually stable in terms of our expectations, they are based on our experience and they cause a certain response. The value will determine the intensity of our reactions because of the importance we attach to the event. You can see how this can affect us. People with certain attitudes and values have a certain kind of personality to go along with it. There are some people who are serious-minded, stubborn and authoritarian. They love emotional control and are quite perfectionistic. These people are diligent and industrious and quite efficient. They seem socially polite, have a high need to achieve and are good organizers. Their value is in their strong sense of duty to others. Their attitude is that one must be conservative, morally and spiritually righteous and have the puritan work ethic. If this is the case you can see where it would lead quickly to a personality with a high need for standards, a high value of work and an automatic predisposition to react to situations quickly when they are different from the attitudes or values that are held by this individual. You can also see that this individual could become quite a compulsive person. We give very little space to this other than to mention that the attitudes and values that we hold automatically determine the first picture that we take of a situation and thus the reaction to that situation. Take for example the following statements:

Men should not wear long hair.

Sex before marriage is wrong.

Men are Smarter than women.

Hard work is the first priority in life.

Christianity is too strict.

Making money is important.

I believe in physical punishment.

Homosexuality is a sin.

It does not take much to recognize that people that hold certain points of view to the statements above will react in certain ways to circumstances surrounding these statements. For example, if you valued and appreciated long hair, you would be friendly and complimentary to a man with long hair. On the other hand, if you felt men should never wear long hair, then you might feel angry or hostile to a man who had long hair.

Your attitudes and values make quite a big difference in terms of how you respond. While we stress this, we also know that attitudes and values are the most difficult things to change. Nevertheless, we must recognize this factor at the outset. Our values and attitudes can produce a lot of stress in our life. We cannot simply ignore them, because these things will come to help us or haunt us as time goes on.

The Symptoms of Stress

In order to help us understand the extent of stress reactions in us, we have prepared a simple stress test. We ask that you have a look at this and make a check mark against any symptoms that apply to you. While we have some scientific evidence that the more symptoms you have, the more stress you experience, we do know that since stress is a highly individual reaction, some people can check off many of these symptoms and still be feeling quite fine, whereas others can have fewer symptoms and not feel well at all. Nevertheless, we ask that you take this stress test. Most symptoms are listed. It is not an exhaustible supply of symptoms, but merely representative of our reactions under stress.

The Stress Symptom Test

Put a checkmark beside any symptom that you have noticed lately in yourself.

PHYSICAL	EMOTIONAL	ATTITUDINAL
• tired	• worry a lot	• empty feeling
• tense	• mood swings	• negative
• can't sleep	• bad dreams	• angry at God
• sleep a lot	• discouraged	• angry at self
• can't eat	• little joy	• angry at others
• eat too much	• cry often	• apathy
• colds, headaches	• temper	• unforgiving
• muscle aches	• don't talk	• self-doubt
• teeth grinding	• talk too much	• cynical attitude
• restless	• angry often	• life goals meanless

SOCIAL	THINKING	PRODUCTIVITY
• fewer friends	• forget things	• work piling up
• stay home more	• can't concentrate	• miss work more
• angry at others	• mind wanders	• pressure at work
• feeling lonely	• think too much	• can't finish up
• lower sex drive	• confused	• no job interest
• manipulative	• think negatively	• procrastinate
• clam up	• feel bored	• work long hours
• afraid to talk	• negatively	• hard to work

You will notice that the stress symptom test has six components. Not all six may be involved in serious stress reactions but most of the time they are. It is true that our body is going to react to stress over time. However, the first reaction is usually emotional. Remember the previous discussion about attitudes. These attitudes that you hold are very stable but their emotional component may change as the stress continues. Over time, you will find the social dimensions affecting you and your productivity at home and at work. If we were to select two categories of symptoms that would be easily identified as first reactions to stress, we would nominate the emotional and the thinking ones. Over an extended period of time, however, the body will begin to react. At first, when stress occurs, you will experience an increased heart rate and an increased breathing rate. When this happens, there will also be a need for increased oxygen consumption, increased glucose, increased blood coagulation and decreased clotting time. Since the heart is involved in a stress reaction, we get increased cardiac stroke volume and increased cardiac output. Pupil dilation, perspiration and increased gastric movements are all bodily reactions to stress.

While we do not intend to be detailed in some of these responses, we do want you to know that the body responds to an aroused system, whether it is pleasant or unpleasant. The effect over time is quite remarkable. For example, under stress the natural body response is to release cortisone from the adrenal glands. This is good because it reduces inflammation, but too much cortisone destroys the body's resistance to many illnesses, including infections and cancer. Too much cortisone also reduces the stomach's resistance to its own acid, thus leading to gastro-intestinal disorders or duodenal ulcers. Another body reaction occurs when the thyroid hormone is increased. This is good because it speeds up body metabolism and burns up its fuel and gives you extra energy, but it also causes shaky nerves, insomnia and the feeling of burnout. Another body reaction is the release of endorphins from the hypothalamus. Endorphins are somewhat like the drug morphine, because they act as natural pain killers and make the body feel good. But chronic stress can deplete the level of endorphins and this is known to aggravate migraines, back aches and arthritis. Under severe stress you can get a shutdown of the entire digestive tract. This is good because now blood can be diverted to the muscles, heart and lungs. You have often seen some people have fantastic feats of strength under stress. The negative reaction is that the mouth goes dry: the stomach and intestines stop secretions. You may have to go to the bathroom more frequently. Most of us have experienced the need to go to the bathroom when we feel anxious. You have also seen public speakers who need glasses of water to speak because their mouth is dry. A dry mouth is used as a lie detector test in some countries in the world. There are other physical reactions to stress. Consult a medical dictionary for the rest. We do know that the blood thickens. This is good because it increases the capacity to carry oxygen and fight infection and to stop bleeding, but it is not good because it can cause strokes and heart attacks. Under stress we also know the skin crawls and sweats. All the senses become more acute. Although this is good because it makes us more sensitive and alert to danger, it is not good because it increases the breathing rate and over-estimates our abilities to cope with the situation. Maybe this list will suffice. At any rate, have a look at your own symptoms of stress and see how well you are faring.

Men and women are known to react differently to stress. This has been researched over and over again. We simply provide a summary of some of that information. The important thing to keep in mind is that both men and women will get sick physically, have headaches, feel tired and may increase some of their bad habits such as smoking and drinking as well as increasing their caffeine intake under stress. What must be understood, though, is the difference in how many men and women experience stress. Men more often experience high blood pressure, heart attack and stroke. Many of the female stress symptoms are related to women's diseases and certainly more women suffer from anorexia and bulimia under stress.

Another major difference in male/female stress symptoms is that some women tend to use more manipulation tactics than others in coping with stress. We have listed four, but there are many others. Mind you, men can practice these manipulation tactics as well as or better than women. Nevertheless, research has listed them under women.

Male and Female Stress Symptoms

Men	*Women*
High Blood Pressure	Anorexia
Muscle Aches	Bulimia
Low Back Pain	Daily Headaches
Daily Headaches	Amenorrhea
Increased Allergies	Sexual Disinterest
Alcoholism	Vaginismus
Ulcers	Infertility
Increased Smoking	Anxiety Reactions
Compulsive Sex	Panic Attacks
Little Sex	Manipulation Tactics
Driving Accidents	• Mind Reading
Motor Habits/Tics	• Grab-bagging
Verbally/Physically Abusive	• Sleuthing
Overeating	• Name-calling
Increased Spending	Increased Dependency
	Depression
	Disorganized

We want to stress once again that our reactions to stress are quite unique. This is important for us to remember because often these unique reactions in and of themselves cause more stress. Take for example the situation where something very bad is happening in your life and your spouse responds to it with greater anxiety, more arousal and more anger than you do. You feel as if your spouse should have reacted the same way as you, given this difficult situation. Now you get upset, not only with this difficult situation, but also with your spouse's reaction to it. We need to understand that no two people are alike. I cannot forget the reactions I saw to a very serious motor vehicle accident on the Sumas Bridge between Chilliwack and Abbotsford. A big semi-truck had just collided with and completely demolished a motor vehicle. There were six people inside the car and they were all killed. The bodies were strewn all over the rain-soaked bridge. As my brother John and I approached the bridge, having parked our car a mile behind the bridge, we saw some people crying and others throwing up. Others were running to the aid and assistance of the people in the car. While nothing could be done for them, they proceeded to cover them up or try to resuscitate them. Some people remain reasonably calm and controlled under stress, while others panic. The different reactions can be physiological and/or experientially based. Nevertheless, they demonstrate that people react very uniquely to stress! If we keep this in mind, we will understand why people react differently to a situation.

The Stages of Stress

We want to mention one final matter with respect to understanding stress. Over time, stress can build up but we'll respond to it in stages. Have a look at a brief summary of these stages:

Stage 1 - Arousal and Irritability
Stage 2 - Fatigue, Cynicism and Withdrawal
Stage 3 - Exhaustion and Collapse

It is important to understand these stages because different things need to be done in each stage. For example, at Stage 1 we are more often irritable, angry and anxious. It is at this stage that we get our headaches and take the pills to control the pain. If we are sensitive enough to our body and mind's reactions to Stage 1, we can pamper ourselves, relax and exercise so as to feel better. If we are not sensitive to these signs, stress will increase and we'll move on to Stage 2.

At Stage 2 we get the feeling of tiredness, cynicism and a negative attitude. Often you will hear people say "I don't care." At Stage 2 we tend to withdraw socially; we feel very tired, yet we can't get to sleep. We begin to procrastinate at work. At Stage 2 our body may physically react to feelings of pain, not just from headaches but from low back pain, increased arthritic pain, increased teeth grinding and other such physical reactions, but the emotional reaction is to become moody and depressed. At this stage, pampering and relaxing may not help as much as making specific changes in our life or learning new stress management skills. It is at this stage that we may have to change our plans and our goals in order to cope.

At Stage 3 we find chronic sadness and depression, extreme fatigue and a dropping out of work and living. It is at this stage that we experience suicide attempts and actual suicides. We often feel like moving away and not giving our forwarding address. This is a stage at which we may need hospitalization and continued long term treatment. At Stage 3 of stress we need to take a break from the pressures of life and get away from it all, at least for a while.

SEASONAL AFFECTIVE DISORDER
also known as
SAD or WINTER DEPRESSION

Hippocrates wrote 2000 years ago that depression often comes on a seasonal basis. Since then there have been many references in the writings of physicians, philosophers, poets and songwriters that depression often occurs in the winter months and may be related to a lack of sunlight. In 1982, Dr. Lewy described the history of an engineer who had fifteen years of mood swings and it was thought that this was related to winter depression. In 1984, Dr. Rosenthal studied 29 patients and described the syndrome "Seasonal Affective Disorder" (SAD). Since that time, many physicians and psychologists from several countries have added to the literature in respect to the disorder which is known as "Seasonal Affective Disorder."

In Dr. Norman Rosenthal's book, "**Seasons of the Mind**", Dr. Rosenthal clearly describes this disorder and gives the names of physicians in North America who work in this area.

The authors of this book have been researching this disorder for the last three years. Our findings were presented to the Canadian Psychiatric Association on October 3, 1991. Our research findings are consistant with other researchers. Here is some information on this disorder.

What are the characteristics of
SEASONAL AFFECTIVE DISORDER?

If you are relatively well during the summer months but require consultation from your physician for the treatment of depression during the winter months, there is a good chance that you are suffering from Seasonal Affective Disorder.

Symptoms

1) Changes in mood. Feelings of sadness, irritability or anxiety.
2) Decreased activity. There is a general feeling of tiredness, weakness and lethargy. No motivation to get things done.
3) Interpersonal difficulties. Because of the feelings of sadness, irritability and anxiety as well as decreased energy, the patient will not get along with other people and tends to pull away.
4) Changes in appetite. In general, there is an increased appetite, a craving for carbohydrates and a tendency to increase weight during winter months.
5) Sleep disturbances. There is a general tendency to go to bed early and sleep for a longer period of time because of this tiredness and exhaustion.
6) Daytime drowsiness. It is hard to keep awake during the daytime and therefore there is a tendency to catnap. There is also a tendency to yawn during the day.
7) Decreased libido or decreased interest in sexual drive.
8) Work difficulties. Because of the drowsiness, decreased energy and mood changes, it is difficult to work at the same or usual level as in the summer months.
9) Exacerbation of menstrual symptoms. The above symptoms tend to worsen just before or during the menstrual period.

Treatment

Patients often blame certain stressors as the cause of their symptoms. Therefore, patients often do not seek consultation from their physician or psychiatrist even when they show some of the above symptoms.

Antidepressants may work effectively for this disorder. These antidepressants may include tricyclics (Desipramine, Imipramine) or Monoamineoxidase Inhibitors such as Parnate or Nardil. A new group of drugs has recently been discovered and seems to work particularly well with few side effects. These drugs are known as the **Selective Serotonin Reuptake Inhibitors (SSRI's)** which include Prozac, Luvox and Zoloft.

One of the most effective treatments for Seasonal Affective Disorder is **bright light therapy**. Bright light therapy consists of using a light box for approximately thirty to sixty minutes each morning. The brightness of the light is

10,000 Lux. A patient should respond to this treatment within four to five days.

The authors have been researching this area and we are treating patients with bright light therapy in Edmonton, Alberta. If you feel that you may have this disorder, it is best that you consult your doctor or psychiatrist. If you are in the Edmonton area, you may want to get involved with our research to see how bright light may improve your disorder.

We are very excited about the research we are doing on a new drug, **Sertraline (Zoloft)**, that has recently been discovered and licensed for sale in Canada. There is evidence that this drug may be effective for individuals suffering from Seasonal Affective Disorder.

"Seasons of the Mind" by Dr. Norman Rosenthal is a complete guide to this disorder and the authors recommend it highly if you are interested in reading more about this disorder.

We included SADS in this chapter on stress because individuals with SADS are in a weakened state. The individual with SADS basically lacks energy. Think of your own experience when you are very tired and have no energy. Now,think of having no energy from November until April. Even the simplest stressors now appear overwhelming. We will never get rid of stress and that's why we need to find ways to cope with it.

Chapter Two

STRESS MANAGEMENT TECHNIQUES

We have said up to this point that control of stress, and management of it, is a very individual thing. Hence, you have to decide which, of all of the following ideas that we will now list, make sense for you. On the other hand, we will argue right at the outset that to be able to manage the daily stressors, you have to make a life style change, much in the same way you have to make a life style change if you want to control your weight. By and large, all stress-coping techniques focus on two things: the first is the problem-focus or instrumental technique and the second is the emotional regulation or the palliative technique. We begin by summarizing the varieties of strategies that will work in most situations. Sometimes stress is simply caused by an emotional reaction to a situation which flares up quickly and dies down just as quickly. If a problem is the cause of stress, then we have to look at the nature of the problem and what to do with it. In the next two paragraphs we will summarize some of the general stress management techniques that will help you solve your problems and help you regulate your emotions. Indeed, the more coping skills you have, the less stress you will experience. Remember, however, that stress is a natural and normal process in life. You should expect it each and every day.

When a problem comes your way, what are the strategies that you could use to try to come to grips with the specific problem? We will list a few ideas:

❖ *Gather information*

Do not react to a problem immediately. Try to say to yourself that before you respond intellectually and emotionally, you will get more information on this. Simply talk to other people or do some reading, and decide that you will not react to this until you have learned more about it.

❖ Communication Skills

It helps to talk through an issue with a trusted friend because it often clarifies your own thinking of the matter. Your friend can also give you some other ideas that may help you think about the problem differently.

❖ Social Skills

People without social skills are usually lonely and under greater stress. We need to find a social support base to assist us in our daily stressors. Developing social skills is a matter entirely unto itself, but it would make sense that you should work on being friendly so that others would be friendly to you.

❖ Time Management

Many problems and stressors in life are caused simply because we have not adequately organized our time. Sometimes this is a matter of personal choice but most of the time we can learn to become better organized. Dr. Paterson and I usually have a day book or calendar with us at all times. We know exactly where we have to be and what we have to do each day. We work at least thirty days in advance so that we can see how booked we are and not overload ourselves. Of course, sometimes conflicts arise or meetings run overtime, but you can allow for this if you use a daily or weekly planner.

❖ Build a Support Base

This is connected to the development of social skills. It is hard to show people how to build a support base. Obviously, those people who are more involved in community service clubs and churches have a wider support base than those who are not. Nevertheless, when the big stressors hit, and you do not have a support base, you find yourself lonely. People without a support base find it more difficult to bounce back.

❖ Leave The Environment

There are circumstances in which one actually has to decide to quit that job, or to leave that marriage, or to walk out of that meeting. We won't say more about it than that. Obviously, it would be a very difficult decision and much more information and planning would have to be made before you actually decided to leave. We keep telling our young adult children never to leave a job until they have the security of another one. Sometimes this is impossible but certainly it would make sense in some circumstances.

❖ Change The Environment

Problems can arise within the home, work and school environment and if one can identify the nature of the problem and make one small change in the system, it would help. Each person has to decide what the specific problem is that is causing the stress and then what changes can be made. Nevertheless, even a small change can reduce stress considerably.

❖ *Problem Solving*

It is amazing how many people do not have a strategy for solving the problem once it comes. We suggest that you first sit down by yourself, or with someone you trust, and try to figure out exactly what the problem is. Next, generate all kinds of possible solutions without criticizing any one of them. Go over each of the listed solutions and decide on the pros and cons of each one. And finally, pick those solutions that make the most sense, and act on them. We think that compromise is always necessary in problem solving. So think about giving in rather than standing firm and being broken in the process.

Coping With Our Emotions

The strategies that we just suggested are useful ideas on how to reduce stress when a problem comes your way. We have not mentioned the wide variety of problem-bases, but some of these will be discussed later in our chapter. For example, we want to talk about the problem of how to pass exams or the problem of how to motivate yourself and study better in college. Keep reading on if that is your circumstance. What we want to focus on next, however, is how to control your emotional reaction under stress conditions. Try some of these ideas:

❖ *Use Denial*

Denial in its simplest form is not admitting to a fault or ignoring the personal involvement within a stress situation. We do not think that use of denial on every occasion is healthy, but there are times when you simply have to push a negative experience out of your memory and actively suppress it.

❖ *Excuses*

If you would like a better term for this you may want to call it rationalization. We all do it. This is a healthy way for us to boost our own self-esteem by giving ourselves all kinds of reasons why the circumstance turned out the way it did. Again, too much use of this technique can cause further problems but there are times when it comes in handy.

❖ *Diversion*

When you find yourself in an anxiety or panic attack it is often easiest to divert your attention to some other pleasurable activity. Talk to yourself and say, "I'm not going to panic but instead I'm going to do an activity that I enjoy."

❖ *Giving Meaning*

This refers to downsizing the problem, as well as the emotion, by telling yourself that this is not the end of the world nor is it as important as your emotions seem to think it is. Use of the self-talk strategy will help you give less meaning to the stress situation, thereby reducing the emotion.

❖ *Distancing*

Distancing simply means that you stand back and remove yourself from the problem. You can begin by telling yourself that while this is causing a reaction in you right now, you are going to stand back and let the arrows of stress pass you by. Distancing can also mean removing yourself from the situation for a while by taking a walk, leaving the room, taking a shower or clamming up. If you make too much use of distancing, friends around you will get worried, but as an immediate control of emotion it works very well.

❖ *Relabelling*

Relabelling means that you talk to yourself and explain the stress situation in a different way to yourself. You do not really need to talk out loud but it helps if you identify the emotion and tell yourself what it is and why this emotion is happening. You can then say that this is not the worst thing that could happen in your life, and that you are not going to react to it as strongly as you feel at the moment.

If we could regulate our emotions effectively, we would probably have super human beings in this world. Nevertheless, the strategies as outlined above all work to some degree. They help in the moment-to-moment emotional calming and make you more capable of looking at the specific problems that may be causing these emotions. Write down the stress-coping techniques above that are more meaningful for you and practice them every day.

Three Life Style Changes

To cope with stress is much like coping with weight loss. Many people are caught by going on a diet, losing weight and then gaining that weight right back again. Their weight goes up and down like a yo-yo. The problem is that they lose weight by losing muscle, as well as some fat, but when they gain the weight back again they do not gain muscle but rather gain fat. Hence there is an even bigger problem the next time they want to go on a diet. Coping with stress acts in a similar manner, unless people make three basic life style changes. The three changes that we suggest are really not that difficult but they must be practised routinely and regularly if they are to work. These life style changes are sensible but not simple. You have to actively decide that from now on you are going to make these changes and then practice them. We suggest them because they work! They organize and regulate your life so that you do not over-react to stress situations.

Change #1: Exercise regularly

Everybody knows that exercise makes sense but as we get older we simply lose interest or we are too tired. We are not suggesting any great big changes in exercise at all. We are simply saying that you must consider that each and every day you should go for a walk, ride a stationary bike, go swimming, or do something else that keeps you active for half an hour. Exercise helps you forget some of your worries. If you exercise enough, your body will produce a chemical that will make you feel better. We call these chemicals endorphins. So sit down and decide exactly what kind of exercise you can do routinely. I have an exercise bike in my bedroom. This is probably the simplest form of workout. You can pedal the bike and read a book or watch a television program at the same time. Try the "buddy system." If you and a friend exercise together you will find that you will exercise more regularly. This is because you support and encourage each other. Whatever it is that you decide to do, decide to exercise every day.

Change #2: Eat Properly

This is neither a book on how to lose weight nor is it simply one on how to eat properly, but proper diet has the effect of making you feel better. The basic premise of eating properly would be to avoid junk food, alcohol and caffeine as much as possible. This is not a surprise to anyone and it should make sense to you. Next we suggest that you reduce salt intake. By doing so, you can reduce your blood pressure as well. This is especially important if you suffer from high blood pressure. Remember that most foods that are processed have a lot of salt in them to begin with, so do not add any more salt to your food. There are also salt substitutes available in health food stores. Look for these and use them regularly. If you do not like the flavour at first, just keep using the substitute and in six months it will taste a lot more like salt to you and you will not mind it at all. Next, we want you to get as much potassium in your system as possible. Potassium serves to help your muscles relax and also helps to control your hypertension. Foods such as bananas, oranges, tomatoes, broccoli, brussel sprouts, carrots, cauliflower, mushrooms, spinach and corn are all reasonably high in potassium. Make sure you have some of these each day.

Magnesium is another substance which actively helps the muscles relax and regulates the heart beat. Look for almonds, beans, brown rice, hazel nuts, oats, peanuts, whole rye and whole wheat bread in particular to increase the intake of magnesium. Calcium is absolutely essential for all of us and especially for women. Calcium can be found in milk products but use those milk products that are low in fat. Cut down on your intake of red meat because this too will control your weight and cholesterol levels. Try eating more chicken and fish and non-animal protein. All of these suggestions are simple enough if you make an active decision to change your eating habits. We know it is may be difficult but over time it will become a habit.

Change #3 - Relaxation

Relaxation can be done in many ways: by exercising, going for a walk, taking a shower, watching a movie, watching television or listening to the radio. What we are suggesting is a 15 to 20 minute exercise that will actively help you relax. I use this relaxation exercise every day. It can be done in your office, home, at recess or in the bathroom. What follows is an actual relaxation technique transcript that involves muscle and mental relaxation in ten easy steps. Read through the physical relaxation exercise as listed below and practice it regularly.

Relaxation Technique #1

This relaxation technique called "**progressive relaxation**" is taken from a program devised by **Dr. Edmond Jacobson**.

Most people feel relaxed the first time they use this technique. But since relaxation is something that can be learned and improved upon, you will find that you will enter into increasingly relaxed states as the process is repeated.

You may also find it helpful to have a friend read the following instructions to you or to make a tape recording of them. Allow plenty of time for completing each step in a comfortable, relaxed manner.

PROGRESSIVE RELAXATION

1. Go to a quiet room with soft lighting. Shut the door and sit in a comfortable chair, feet flat on the floor, eyes closed.

2. Become aware of your breathing.

3. Take in a few deep breaths, and as you let out each breath, mentally say the word, "relax."

4. Concentrate on your face and feel any tension in your face and eyes. Make a mental picture of this tension (it may be a rope tied in a knot or a clenched fist) and then mentally picture it relaxing and becoming comfortable, like a limp rubber band.

5. Experience your face and eyes becoming relaxed. As they relax, feel a wave of relaxation spreading throughout your body.

6. Tense your eyes and face, squeezing tightly, then relax them and feel the relaxation spreading throughout your body.

7. Apply the previous instructions to other parts of your body. Move slowly down your body: jaw, neck, shoulders, back, upper and lower arms, hands, chest, abdomen, thighs, calves, ankles, feet, toes. Do this until every part of your body is relaxed. For each part of the body, mentally picture tension, then picture the tension melting away; tense the area then relax it.

8. When you have relaxed each part of the body, rest quietly in this comfortable state for two to five minutes.

9. Then let the muscles in your eyelids lighten up, become ready to open your eyes, and become aware of the room.

10. Now let your eyes open, and you are ready to go on with your usual activities.

If you have not already done so, we encourage you to go through this process before reading on. You can find the relaxation it produces pleasurable and energizing. People sometimes experience difficulty keeping their minds from wandering the first few times they try the process. There is no need to feel discouraged. It is very natural, and criticizing yourself will only increase your tension.

There is another form of relaxation exercise that we like to practice with small or large groups whenever we give speeches. This relaxation technique involves forming pictures in your head. It is a visual relaxation technique. The transcript of this technique is as follows:

Relaxation Technique #2

SIT BACK & CLOSE YOUR EYES.

Take a deep breath and let that breath out slowly. Feel yourself relax all over as you close your eyes and breath deeply and regularly. Do this for a few minutes. Make sure you are comfortable on your chair and your head is supported so that it does not topple over as you get deeply relaxed. Just sit back, breathe deeply and let the air out slowly. Imagine that you can see your lungs filling up with air inside. See it fill up your lungs completely and then watch the air level go down in your lungs as you let the air out very slowly.

NOW imagine yourself sitting in a classroom that you were once in many years ago. There are a number of desks in the classroom, a blackboard at the front and a teacher's desk. Just continue to sit back and relax. Breathe deeply and let the air out slowly. Relax, let go, and relax.

NOW I want you to go up to the blackboard. There is a chalk ledge there and a piece of chalk. I want you to pick up that chalk and draw a circle on the blackboard. Now I want you to look on the chalk ledge and there you will see an eraser. Pick up the eraser and erase the circle that you have drawn on the blackboard. Now stand back and tell me what you see on the blackboard.

NOW go back to your seat and relax. Continue to breathe deeply and slowly and let all your muscles in your body relax. Breathe deep and easy, easy and relax. Now I want you to look to the teacher's desk. On it is a vase of flowers.

Can you see the flowers? The flowers are many and beautiful. Look at those flowers and tell me what colour they are.

NOW continue to breathe deeply and relax. Slow and easy, quiet and relaxed.

NOW I want you to go up to that teacher's desk and smell the flowers. The final question is, "Can you smell the flowers?"

NOW go back to your desk, sit down and relax. After a few moments I want you to slowly open your eyes and scan the room where you are sitting so that you can become more fully awake. Look around and shake your shoulders and your arms, hands and legs. When you are fully awake, get up and stretch and then go about your daily duties.

This exercise tells us as group leaders just the extent to which visualization is important in helping you relax. There are some people that simply cannot visualize and so they have to use the muscle or physical relaxation exercises that we described previously. Those of you who are good at visual imagery can use this procedure. You can visualize yourself in any place that you find relaxing, such as a beach, a forest area or any other place. Practice this exercise every day. You will find it a calming experience.

Short Term Stress Reduction Strategies

How to pamper yourself within your budget! Here are a few suggestions:

★ *Go for a 1 km walk*

   ★ *Take a hot bath, shower*

★ *Get a legitimate massage*

   ★ *Listen to relaxation tapes*

★ *Start doodling and keeping a diary*

   ★ *Buy yourself a small gift*

★ *Book a weekend somewhere*

   ★ *Listen to music after work*

★ *Stop watching the news on TV*

   ★ *Prepare yourself for romance and sex*

★ *Book time for your hobby*

   ★ *Plan an evening out with friends*

★ *Begin a small renovation project*

   ★ *Take an evening class of interest*

★ *Read in your interest area*

   ★ *Do some volunteer work*

★ *Meditate and pray each day*

   ★ *Get yourself a pet*

★ *Book off early once a week*

   ★ *Take your spouse to a movie, play*

★ *Learn to bake from scratch*

   ★ *Daydream before sleep*

The idea of "pampering yourself within your budget" comes from Dr. Peter Hanson's book *The Joy of Stress*, a book that we have mentioned previously. Have a look at the suggestions listed above. Pick those that are particularly important for you and begin to practice them. I have found that while some things work for me, others do not. I find it important to plan an evening out with friends, read in my interest area, do some volunteer work, meditate and pray each day. Dr. Paterson finds it helpful to take a hot shower, play with his dogs or take his spouse to a movie or a play. Whatever works for you, do it. We find it absolutely essential that you also look at the idea of booking a weekend somewhere. We think that it helps our stress to be able to plan a weekend trip once every three months. Plan it well in advance and go on a trip that you can afford and look forward to. Whatever the ideas that you come up with in addition to ours, make the changes now. We know that these ideas are short term because they do not get rid of the problem causing the stress. However, it will certainly reduce the emotional impact of the stress. If you have a plan for a brief vacation once every 12 weeks, you will find yourself reacting more calmly to the daily stressors of living.

How to Make Worrying Work For You

Try these ideas!

▼ You can't quit worrying, so do not try!

▼ Think of the positives of worrying:
>   Increases vigilance
>   Forces change
>   Motivates
>   Moves you to problem-solve

▼ Identify the issues - get to the point
>   Do not worry in the abstract
>   Write down possible solutions

▼ Now write down possible solutions

▼ If solutions are hard to find, talk to a trusted friend

▼ If worry still persists, use the "worry chair"
>   Decide to worry once a day
>   Choose a worry place and time
>   Now sit down and worry
>   Stop after 20 minutes
>   Now distract yourself in any way
>   Decide to worry again next day,
>   same time, same place

Everyone worries! We know that it is impossible to stop worrying entirely but there are strategies to use so that you can control it. Go through the six points listed above and read them very carefully. Now use the worry chair just the way we have suggested it. While you are sitting in this chair remember that you can not quit worrying so do not try. Sit in the chair and think of the good parts of worrying as noted in the second point above. As you are sitting there in a relaxed way, try to think of the issues. Remember never to worry in the abstract. That is, do not say, "What am I going to do? This is terrible...I can't take it...This is impossible...What is going to happen next?" If you like, write down each worry and now write down possible solutions. If the worry still persists, you can sit in that worry chair and worry actively for as long as you can. We think it is almost impossible to worry for longer than five to ten minutes but try that and see what happens. You will find that as you choose your place of worrying in that chair you will worry less the rest of the day.

It is important for you to choose a place in the home that is not a room that you find pleasant. In other words, do not put the worry chair in your bedroom, living room, family room or kitchen but rather in some other place that is quite different, that you do not go to regularly. Put the chair there, sit down and worry. Try this strategy if you are a big worrier.

Long Term Stress Reduction Strategies

We have given you a lot of ideas on how to cope with stress that are basic stress management but most of these are short term. While we think that exercise, diet and relaxation in and of themselves will be very helpful to you on a daily basis and that these short term ideas will be useful in controlling emotions as well as worry, there has to be some further thought as to how to handle stress on a long term basis. This is especially true if we have some very big problems in our lives that will take years to change. What we are suggesting in this following action plan is a five step procedure that will help you come to grips with major issues that are causing stress in your life. Have a look at this action plan:

The Stress Coping Action Plan

Step 1   Work on a balance in life style
                        Home
                        Health
                        Work
                        Social
                        Spiritual
          Sit Down and Take Stock
Step 2   Avoid Impulsive, Radical Changes
          e.g.   Moving, Quitting, Divorce
Step 3   Now Choose Long-Term Coping Strategies
          e.g.   Communication Skills
                  Job Skills
                  Plan Each Day, Week, Month
                  Act Out of Caring For You and Others
                  Acclaim Your Achievements
                  Acclaim The Average
Step 4   Now Add Positive Addictions
          e.g.   Delegate Your Power
                  Remove the Quick Fixes (coffee, alcohol)
                  Regularize Exercise
                  Hobbies
                  Noontime Catnaps
                  Add Social, Family Time
Step 5   Put all this in writing and read it often.

We state in Step 1 that you have to work on a balance in your life style, a balance between five major factors. Some time has to be set aside in your calendar or day book to practice healthy living by eating and exercising and relaxing. Nevertheless, we think that the first step in a long-term plan is to sit down and take stock. Successful businessmen like John D. Rockefeller have utilized this first step in changing their life around and reducing the stress. We are busy, hard-working people. We often find that our work tires us out so much that we have relatively little energy to put into our family and home. Friends go by the wayside and we are too tired to worry about exercising or eating right. Many of us are involved in church activities, but not all of us are concerned about the spiritual side of life. What we are suggesting is that you actively work on balancing the amount of time you put into one area as opposed to another. If you can back off on work and spend more time at home or with friends then do it! A change has to be planned and discussed with significant others in your life before it actually happens. Taking stock is an exercise that could be done on one of the weekend trips that you are taking. Find ways in which you can work fewer hours but with time management accomplish more than you did before. Actively plan time with the spouse or children on weekends.

We know that successful marriages are those in which 87% of the time on weekends is spent with the family or with the spouse. Book in your times for exercise and relaxation and also book in time for friends. If you are involved in church activities, do not allow that to overtake your life either. While church is very important, it too can just be another stress factor in your life giving you more to do. You may have to learn to say "no" sometimes and this is a good time to do it.

Our long-term action plan first involves sitting down and taking stock and working out a balance in life style. From then on we make some suggestions that are very helpful. We know that avoiding impulsive, radical changes as listed above is absolutely essential. It is absolutely essential because during times of stress we are more prone to make impulsive changes. We may notice that a relative has been very annoying and stressful to us, for example. So we may impulsively decide to "tell that relative off." However, this may bring more problems than we had to begin with. It may have been better to think the problem through and decide to simply decrease our involvement with that relative. So simply decide that no immediate change will happen when we are under stress. Tell yourself and others that you will take time to think and plan before you make any changes. Go to a counsellor or to a trusted friend and discuss any changes. Gather information, write down the pros and cons and then make decisions once the stress level has gone down.

Now it's time to choose the long-term coping strategies. We list several of them. Long-term means that we practice them from now on until the day we die! Notice that we are talking about improving communication skills and job skills. Plan each day very carefully on your calendar and make up your mind to act out of caring for yourself and others. Each and every day you should acclaim your achievements and be satisfied with just being average. After all, we are just average! It is a common foible to look for the greener grass on the other side of the mountain. It is natural for us to want to achieve but we think it is equally important just to be satisfied with who we are and what we have. We call this 'acclaiming the average.' This takes very active self-talk to say, "I'm okay with what I have and what I do. I do not need that extra car, television or motor home. I am pleased with the home that I have at the moment. I am satisfied with the accomplishments that I have to date." Satisfaction within your budget is also acclaiming the average.

We still believe entirely in dreams and visions and if you plan to follow a dream, you can make it happen. But in the meantime, be satisfied with what you have and where you are. This is a long-term thing. If you practice it actively, it will work for you.

Now look at step 4 and add your positive addictions. Notice the first example is 'delegating your power.' Many people feel that "if I do it myself it gets done," but you have to give up some of your activities by letting others help. Positive addictions such as noon-time catnaps and fun family time should have already happened in Step 1 of the Stress Coping Action Plan. Sit down and write out your plan. Do it now!

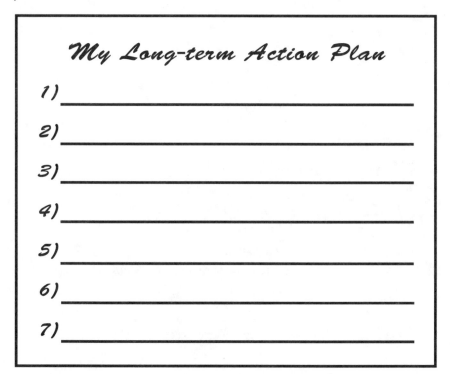

My Long-term Action Plan

1) _____

2) _____

3) _____

4) _____

5) _____

6) _____

7) _____

The Power of Positive Thinking

Most of us know about Norman Vincent Peale and have read his books. There are few people in this world that would not agree that positive thinking is a helpful thing. What we are suggesting is another major long-term strategy: to change the way we think. There are ways that you can keep yourself fresh, alive and enthusiastic. But there are other ways that people can certainly keep themselves from being positive and effective. We can say that change is disruptive and disturbing. How many times have you said "Ain't it awful?" People find themselves whining and complaining. Often, before I go into a school staff room I feel pretty good, but after hearing all the complaining going on I feel rotten. Whining, moaning and groaning de-energizes us and increases our stress. What we would like to do now is to list positive thinking techniques that you will find easy to do once you practice them.

Positive Thinking Strategies

STOP

De-energizing behaviours

Us against them
Moaning and groaning
Procrastination
Always looking back
Attributing power to others
Blame self or others

START

Energizing yourself

Realize you have options
Focus on a better world
Confront your problems
Reward yourself
Focus on the here and now
Exercise and enjoy activities
Confide in others
Introspect and risk

You will notice that in the first part of the above list we want you to stop those behaviours that make you feel rotten and miserable. We have already mentioned the whining and complaining and the "awfulizing." We also want you to stop this feeling of 'us against them' because the emphasis on competition, while helpful in one way, is de-energizing in another way. An emphasis on competition is another way for people to make themselves unhappy. When we become competitive, we burn up some of our energy in the struggle and less of our attention can be directed toward the work tasks for which we are accountable. Always looking back to the past is another way to feel rotten because the past, under stress, always seems to look darker than it really was. So stop looking back and look forward instead. Also, stop attributing power to others. We often moan and groan with friends and colleagues, thereby reinforcing our own dejection and depression. We often say, "If only I didn't have such a rotten boss I wouldn't feel so bad." When we say this we are attributing a tremendous amount of power to that boss. It is possible to attribute power to other people that they do not have. If you think that somebody else has too much influence and there is nothing you can do about it, you are attributing power to that person: adding power to what he or she already has. It is 'an unhappy syndrome' that prevents a person from doing things he does well and from making positive choices. Stop blaming yourself or others for your troubles or putting the blame for everything that happens on your shoulders. Either way you decrease your energy and make yourself feel greater stress.

While we want you to stop de-energizing behaviours we want you to start thinking positively and energize yourself. Begin by thinking about the options that you have. Even when times are very tough and the situation very difficult, there are always options. You may not like the options but they are still options. And just knowing that there is an option is a freeing experience. You can tell yourself that you choose to stay in the running. Say, "I choose the work I am doing, the boss I have, the place I am living, the salary I am earning." Convincing yourself that life is your choice gives you a sense of control.

Start thinking of the good things in this world. Think of the fact that it is a better world with less disease, better organizations, better food availability, better transportation and better communication than ever before. One can think optimistically instead of negatively. On the other hand, you should not plan too much or "bite off more than you can chew." A person's plans can be broken down into little bits - small steps instead of huge ones. It is possible to reach a goal by taking one step at a time. We also know it is easier to confront your problems and assert yourself than to ignore them. While we have said that denial and excuses are short-term strategies and helpful to reduce emotions, we also know that it takes more energy to do these things than to actively confront. It is not necessary to shout at that person who is causing you difficulty; just acknowledge a problem that needs some work. Confront carefully and tenderly. It works better to say, "I'd like to talk to you about the silly habit you have of picking your nose," instead of, "Grab a brain. You look like an idiot when you pick your nose." In general, it takes less energy to confront than not to confront.

While it seems simple to be able to reward yourself each day, it does take practice and training. Since your accomplishments may be known only to you, others may not be able to reinforce your achievements. Reward yourself: take some time off, give yourself a gift or tell a friend. Boasting or claiming credit for a job well done is an energizing activity, as long as it does not become bragging.

From now on we want you to focus on the here and now. If you enjoy that time of relaxation or that discussion with a friend, tell yourself so and tell the friend. Let your hair down and tell others exactly what is bothering you. You can use your energy at that moment to be positive. Remember, we have already said that it is important to take time for sufficient recreation and simply shutting off the motor. True confiding in other people and letting them know some of your feelings, worries and wants is a positive and not a negative force. While it makes you vulnerable, it also strengthens you because a trusted friend can come up with some solutions if necessary, or at least support you in your feelings. If you keep secrets inside yourself, there is a good chance you can make yourself sick. While some secrets may need to be kept, most do not. Everyone knows people who have ulcers because they keep everything to themselves.

Self analysis helps, too. People can stop and analyze why they are upset, what is really the fear, and, if that fear actually happened, whether or not it would be the end of the world. Remember, looking at yourself honestly and realistically is a good thing to do. There is no sense in the "ostrich technique," where you simply bury your head in the sand and forget about those things that you can do well or those things you can not do well. Look carefully inside yourself and look for the positive. Do those things you can do.

Remember that you are more than just body. Remind yourself that you have a mind, but you are not just mind. Remind yourself that you have feelings but are not just feelings, either. You are all of these things. You are a body, a mind and feelings - and a great deal more. Each person has a higher self. You can put yourself in a different perspective; you are not trapped inside what you understand in your mind; you can transcend your mind and look into things you do not comprehend. Everything does not have to make sense. If you insist on experiencing only what you understand, then you are narrowing your world. Your choices stem from your own sense of personal potency and your caring about others. When you make those choices from the centre of your higher self, they are better for you and for the others in your life.

The great poet Longfellow once said:

> *"Not in the clamour of the crowded street,*
>
> *not in the plaudits of the throng,*
>
> *but in ourselves,*
>
> *are triumphs and defeats."*

Realistic Self-Talk

Self-talk, the messages we give ourselves, can greatly affect the way we feel. For example, when I say to myself, "You did a fine job," I feel good inside. When I tell myself, "You botched it, you idiot!" I feel quite differently.

Much anxiety is initiated and maintained by the self-clobbering and irrational messages we give ourselves. This self-talk not only creates anxiety and bad feelings, it also distracts us from the task at hand and makes it harder to succeed.

Fortunately, there are ways to control destructive self-talk and to replace it with nurturing, realistic, on-task messages that are productive and self-enhancing. Non-productive self-talk is a mental habit. By practising the four-step procedure outlined below, new and more constructive habits of self-talk can be developed.

STEP 1. IDENTIFY DESTRUCTIVE SELF-TALK

Destructive self-talk is usually one of two kinds: self-clobbering or irrational.

A. Self-clobbering messages usually take the form of belittling "you" statements. For example:

"You dummy."

"You should have known better."

"Can't you do anything right?"

"You're ugly."

"You're silly."

"You're weak."

"You can't control yourself."

"You do not have any confidence."

"You're never going to amount to anything."

"You can't do this."

You know that a clobbering message has hit home and taken effect when you find yourself feeling bad, and sadly or anxiously agreeing: "I'm dumb," "I can't do this" or "I'll never amount to anything."

B. Irrational self-talk comes from the illogical and unreasonable ideas many of us have about different situations. These beliefs, which are learned early in life and often supported by our culture, cause unnecessary emotional turmoil. For example:

"If I do not do well on this test, I'll flunk out of school and be a failure in life."

"In order to be worthwhile, I have to be completely competent, adequate, intelligent, and successful in everything I do."

"If someone dislikes me or disapproves of me, I'm no good."

"If I seem out of control or not confident, people will not respect me and that would be awful."

"I have no control over myself."

STEP 2. STOP DESTRUCTIVE SELF-TALK

We human beings have control over what we focus on and think about. For example, if you desire to focus on an object, you can turn your attention to it. You can also turn your attention away from an object and onto something else. Here are two methods for turning your focus away from destructive self-talk.

A. Gentle method:

In a nurturing way, say to yourself something like: "I do not want to clobber myself right now. That just hurts me and makes me feel bad. I'll turn my attention to something else," or "I do not want to scare myself with this irrational idea." The important idea here is to adopt a caring and respectful tone toward self.

B. Firm method:

In cases where the gentle method fails to work and the self-defeating messages persist, you can "yell" at yourself internally (without making an audible noise): "STOP IT!" With this method you can jolt yourself away from even the most persistent irrational or clobbering message. Then take a deep breath or two and gently turn to more nurturing, rational messages. Important note: Do not clobber yourself (e.g., Stop it, you jerk!).

STEP 3. INITIATE RATIONAL, NURTURING SELF-TALK

By repeatedly replacing destructive self-talk with more constructive messages, new mental habits can be established which promote confidence and productivity.

A. Nurturing messages help us counteract self-clobbering, feel good about ourselves, and approach life's tasks more confidently. In giving ourselves these messages, we should be as realistic as possible, avoiding both false modesty and exaggerations of our positive qualities. To be effective these messages should be positive and believable. For example:

"I'm an intelligent person."

"I make mistakes, but I'm not going to make the same ones over and over."

"I'm not perfect, but I'm a good person."

"When I sit down to do something, I can usually accomplish it."

"I can control what I do."

"I can do this."

"There's nothing awful about me."

B. Rational messages can counteract the anxiety and pressure fostered by irrational self-talk. As with nurturing messages, rational self-talk should be positive in tone, believable, and often practised. For example:

"Doing poorly on a test isn't the end of the world. I do not want to
scare myself unnecessarily."

"If someone doesn't like me, it may hurt for a while, but it doesn't mean
I'm not a good person."

"Everyone makes mistakes. I may be disappointed, but I'll live through it."

"I can control what I do."

STEP 4. GIVE YOURSELF ON-TASK INSTRUCTIONS

In addition to provoking bad feelings, clobbering and irrational self-talk distracts us from the task at hand, divides our energies and makes it more difficult to do our best. The final step in this process is to direct ourselves back to the task in a nurturing way. For example:

"I do not want to clobber myself anymore; it's best for me to get back
to reading this chapter. I'll just take it one section at a time."

"I do not want to scare myself with this irrational idea any more.
I want to listen to what this person is saying."

Reversing Destructive Behaviours

What are Habits?

When the co-hosts of "That's Living" talked about habits on radio, people tended to want to disagree with any point of view that was expressed. There is a continuing debate in the literature as to the difference between a habit and an addiction. Does the heavy smoker or compulsive eater have a bad habit or an addiction? For purposes of this topic, we will simply call a habit an automatic response. Few would disagree that we perform many routine tasks each and every day out of habit. Most people will put on either their left shoe or their right shoe first; we do not make a conscious decision each time we get dressed.

What are Destructive Habits?

Some people reading this will expect me to talk about smoking, so I will not disappoint them. Smokers who are endangering their health have a destructive habit. In fact, in view of recent scientific evidence, it is difficult to think of any smoker who does not contribute to some form of destructive situations like heart disease or second-hand smoke, not to mention lung damage. But many other minor habits can be destructive: eating too much, biting your nails, clearing your throat, chewing ice or strumming your fingers on a table. However, I think each person involved may have to be consulted to find out what is a destructive habit. Some people drink every week, without this seeming to effect either work or family. Others drink occasionally and it has become a serious problem in their lives. Any habit that is done without conscious thought and which bothers an individual or others around can be said to be destructive. This can also lead to stress.

What Not to Do!

Will Power

It would be wonderful if every person could experience the same thoughts and emotions as every other person. I am sure, for example, that every reformed smoker can give an easy and useful way for others to stop smoking. The difficulty is that what works for one individual will not necessarily work for another. When we tell people "use will power," we are probably making the situation worse, not better.To suggest to somebody that a bad habit is simply a case of will power indicates that we do not understand the problem. Some people smoke because they are lonely, others eat because they do not like their physical appearance. Some bite their nails because they are frustrated, anxious, fearful and upset. Looking to find problem areas and working towards solutions is more useful than simply saying, "It is a question of will power." This insensitive remark is usually not helpful.

Giving Advice

Advice does not work either. The American psychologist Thomas Gordon once indicated, in talking about assumptions of human behaviour, that it is almost impossible to change behaviour by simply pointing out mistakes and giving advice. I agree with that premise. It is too bad in a way, because many of our educational strategies are based on the assumption that if we give people information that those people will change their behaviour. We know that does not work. Admonitions like, "You can do better if you try" usually have little influence on a child's educational career for example. Advice to adults such as, "You must stop gambling" or "You are underweight, eat more," often fall on deaf ears. To help people reverse destructive habit patterns means we need to understand each and every individual, rather than relying on time-honoured maxims.

Self-Image and Habit Control

There are strategies, though, that do work. Psychologists have long known that a person's self- image is very important when that individual makes decisions about life situations. That is, some of us see ourselves as thin, or young, or athletic, or whatever. Our own picture of our physical appearance and personality often reflects the decisions we make in day-to-day situations. One way to stop a person from smoking is to convince that person first that he or she is a non-smoker. If I truly believe that I am a non-smoker and that I am in control of this habit, then every time I light a cigarette it is difficult for me and it forces me to think about it. Conscious thought is an enemy to habit formation.

Much of the work done in counselling has to do with making people recognize strengths and developing strategies in day-to-day life situations that fit their perceived strengths in personality development. A person who drinks or gambles might be able to perceive that he or she is in a temporary "rut." Next month or next year will be the time to move forward. If any individual truly believes that a habit can be controlled, then it can.

Emphasis on Positives

It stands to reason that the more accurate our self-image is, the more likely we will be able to utilize that concept in making behaviour changes. If we are to help someone reverse a habit, we must first know that person. Let us know what Mary or George really wants in life, then we can assist in pointing out that a destructive habit is blocking rather than facilitating short and long-term goals. The food addict who loses two pounds in a week must be encouraged for that positive sign, rather than reminded of a still grossly overweight situation. The comment "you catch more flies with honey than vinegar" is true. People will work on habit control if they see success; if a person builds in an excuse before starting a change in habit structure, then the destructive habit will remain. For example, if while trying to lose weight I said, "I may not be able to lose weight now because I am working hard and I am stressed out." Let us face it, when are we not under some form of stress?

Now and Later

Sometimes a habit can have such an intensity that a person is controlled by it. Some people who wish to lose weight believe that if they could lose between twenty and thirty pounds, the world would be different. Unfortunately, weight loss takes time, so in reality people seeing that individual on a day-to-day basis will not even notice the change. If you want to change habits think about what you would do differently if you did not have a particular problem. For example, an individual trying to lose weight might want to buy a bathing suit as if the weight loss had already occurred. Build in the reward while you are working on the habit control, not necessarily afterwards. If a person plans a holiday after stopping smoking, they should go in the early stages of their stop smoking scenario. If an individual thinks thin or thinks like a non-smoker, the rest will follow, often with professional assistance.

How to Change Habit Patterns

STEP 1. Assisting a person in habit control means that you must first learn about the person, not the habit. We help more people if we focus on the person rather than working only on problems.

STEP 2. If a person has a destructive habit, assist that individual in learning to relax. People can relax in many ways: exercise, swimming, card playing, having a hot bath, etc. If people are going to be truly able to change life patterns, they must be able to relax.

STEP 3. Try to develop short-term attainable goals in some kind of "fun" fashion. Do not say, "Tomorrow I will be a non-smoker"; instead, talk about cutting back fifty percent and then rewarding yourself for that achievement. Remember that you can have fun in other ways besides maintaining a destructive habit.

STEP 4. Anticipate and hope for initial early success. This means that we don't want to set the goals too high. If you are a gambler and you do not gamble for a week, that is great! This is probably better than statements like, "I will never gamble again" which can be broken at every conceivable opportunity.

STEP 5.   Once you have decided that you are going to do something about your destructive habit, an excellent first step would be to consult your doctor. The next step is doing all the things that you know will help you to achieve your goal.

STEP 6.   Keep your sense of humour. You will need it!

How to Achieve A Positive Self-Image

Self-image is what we think of ourselves, self-esteem is how much we value or like ourselves. You may consider yourself a good singer, mechanic, ball player or cook. This is your self-image. The psychological self-esteem is when you really like yourself and feel good about the kind of person you are. Often the two terms are used interchangeably, but there is a subtle difference.

Have an accurate but positive point of view about yourself.
This is important! If a person had below average marks all through school, even though they worked very hard, careers as a brain surgeon or nuclear scientist are probably not feasible. It is important that if we learn from experience, we must know something about our own strengths and limitations. So while it is important that we have an accurate view about what we can and cannot do, we must also be positive and look for ways in which we can improve ourselves. It is too stressful to reach beyond our capabilities.

Be realistic.
When teaching students to become counsellors, I have often warned them to be careful about encouraging students to "turn over a new leaf." Sometimes we get discouraged with the way we are and try to change too many things at once. A high school student making grades in the 40% range will not likely improve this average to 90% in a short period of time. What often happens when we make radical changes is that we try for a short period of time, become discouraged, then stop. While each of us should look for ways to improve, let us improve slowly with short-term as well as long-term goals. We must take one small step at a time!

Encourage and enjoy positive interactions with others.

Human culture is group culture. The way we find out about who we are is by what others tell us about ourselves. If we think about it for a minute, it is difficult for us to even have an accurate idea of our physical appearance, never mind our mental abilities or personalities. We rely on others to tell us who we are. It is for this reason that a child who grows up in a loving and caring home is emotionally healthier than a child who faces adversity throughout life. A loving and nurturing home develops a child's ability to say, "They like me. I am a nice person. I feel good about myself." On the other hand, a hostile environment or an environment that is non-nurturing or non-supportive leads the child to feel, "I never do anything right. No one likes me. I better watch out or I will get hit again. I wish I could run away." If we are to receive positive feedback, it makes sense that we should give positive feedback. If an individual is seen as a positive and helpful person, that feedback will be relayed back to us. While it does not quite fit, the next quotation is close: "Do unto others as you would have them do unto you." In any event, can we ever do better than following the Golden Rule?

Engage in a wide variety of activities so negatives in one area will not distort your view of self.

Are you a workaholic? When things go badly in the work setting, are you devastated? Do you know anyone like this? It stands to reason that if you can see yourself operating in a wide variety of settings like in the family, a work setting, church, recreational pursuits or community activities, then when there is difficulty in one area you do not assume to be somehow a total failure. You can be successful in one area, and unsuccessful in another. This book is full of maxims but the following applies: "Do not put all your eggs in one basket."

Control envy.

Remember your school days? When you wrote a very difficult examination and thought you might have failed, you would have given anything to be guaranteed that you would receive a B or an average mark. When the mark came back and you found you had a B but were very close to an A, you were disappointed, rather than pleased. It is a sad fact of life that people who have five million dollars are often envious of those who have eight or ten million. While it is good to strive and improve, it is important, if we are to like ourselves, that we are satisfied with modest gains and improvements, rather than always looking for role models who are wealthier, brighter, and more attractive.

Boast sometimes. We hear ourselves as well as others.

Earlier we noted that human culture is group culture. Let us not forget we are part of that culture. If you have a wonderful child, or grandchild, or you have participated in any notable achievement, let somebody know. When we talk positively about ourselves, we are also listening. It is nice to be humble, but we should sometimes talk about those things we like about ourselves like our family or our achievements.

Be yourself.

Do you remember your job interview? If you were like me, you sat and tried to think of what the employer wanted to hear. It became a very artificial situation. There has to be a first time for every situation, but we act as if we have been there before. If we trust ourselves and our instincts, it will be better than changing our behaviour to please others. If you like yourself, then be yourself.

Do not clobber yourself for engaging in destructive self-talk or destructive behaviours. Nurture yourself, build up your self-image and be patient. With time and practice, you will gradually break these self-defeating mental habits and free

STAYING ON TOP

All are architects of Fate,
*   Working in these walls of Time;*
Some with massive deeds and great,
*   Some with ornaments of rhyme.*

Nothing useless is, or low;
*   Each thing in its place is best;*
And what seems but idle show
*   Strengthens and supports the rest.*

For the structure that we raise,
*   Time is with materials filled;*
Our todays and yesterdays
*   Are the blocks with which we build.*

Build today, then, strong and sure,
*   With a firm and ample base;*
And ascending and secure
*   Shall tomorrow find its place.*

Thus alone can we attain
*   To those turrets, where the eye*
Sees the world as one vast plain,
*   And one boundless reach of sky.*

- Henry Longfellow (The Builder)

Longfellow's words "Our todays and yesterdays are the blocks with which we build" is indeed true. The central idea relates to lifestyle risk factors. You may be acquainted with this term but I think it is worth repeating so that we can work on our todays and yesterdays in a manner that will build towards our future.

Working in the hospital day after day and year after year I witness terrible personal tragedies, as individuals and their families deal with illness or accidents. Many of these tragedies could have been prevented. Let me give you an example. Recently I was asked to consult a patient who was severely depressed. When I came to the patient's bedside, I introduced myself and told the patient that I was a psychiatrist and was asked to examine the patient in respect to depression. The attending physician was concerned that the depression was severe and may need treatment. It did not take long for the patient to tell me about his depressive feelings, and then to say, "This is all due to my stupidity. I knew I should have stopped smoking years ago. They now tell me that my lung cancer has spread to different parts of my body and is untreatable."

It is a medical fact that nine out of ten people who develop lung cancer do so directly as a result of smoking. We therefore use the concept of life stye risk factors to mean, "If part of my lifestyle is to smoke, then I am risking the development of lung cancer." It really does not take a lot of intellect to know that this individual with his untreatable lung cancer can no longer STAY ON TOP.

My message is quite simple. One way of staying on top is to maintain our health at the highest possible level. One way of maintaining health is to educate ourselves as much as we can about life style risk factors. I encourage you to find information about how to keep yourself healthy.

Let us look at another example. Recently Alberta enacted a seat belt law. It has been established for many years that seat belts reduce injury and reduce the number of deaths that occur due to motor vehicle accidents. Also, we know from traffic statistics that at least fifty per cent of all motor vehicle accidents are directly caused by an intoxicated driver. Fortunately, the number of impaired drivers has dropped for seven consecutive years in Alberta and 1990 was the lowest level in the past fifteen years. Without any doubt, this was related to public education and special programs developed by the local police department. It is well known that speed kills. How many times have we driven without using our seat belt? How many times have we driven while we were intoxicated? How many times did we speed? To restate my central thesis, there are certain life style risk factors in relationship to driving. These are speeding, drinking and not using the seat belt. If we choose to carry out a life style that will put us at risk, then the end result is quite clear. We will be injured or dead.

If we are injured: we have pain, we require medical care, we are unable to go to work, we will be unable to socialize and our finances will suffer because of the direct costs of the accident, our medical care, and the possibility of loss of job. By carrying out a life style which includes speeding, driving while intoxicated or not using our seat belt, we increase our chances to develop stress.

We often use the "mechanism of denial." That is, we say such things as, "It will not happen to me" or "I am in a hurry and there is nobody else on the highway so I can speed." It therefore follows that if we do not know about the idea of life style risk factors in relationship to motor vehicle accidents, or if we use denial, we will not recognize that we are carrying out destructive behaviour and therefore we will not do anything to reverse these destructive behaviours.

Let me present one more example. The statistics for 1991 in respect to breast cancer in women show that one in ten women will develop breast cancer in their lifetime. Every year 14,400 Canadian women are diagnosed with breast cancer. At the present time, the only thing that we can do about breast cancer is to attempt prevention by early diagnosis. Dr. Susan Love in her book "**Breast Book**" states that the breast self-examination technique can detect about eighty-five per cent of all lumps. Dr. Love also states that the mammogram can detect tumours one millimetre across (one tenth to one twentieth the size of tumours that are normally detected by self-examination). If we try and put these statistics and statements to my central thesis, we can say that a woman's life style should consist of regular self-examination of breasts, annual examinations by a physician and a mammogram on an annual basis after the age of fifty. Therefore, if a woman carries out a life style which includes these examinations of the breast, then she will more likely be able to detect the cancer at a very early stage, maintain her health and stay on top. She will have less stress, too. On the other hand, women who do not understand the life style risk factors of not examining their breasts will not be able to detect the breast cancer early, will require intensive medical treatment, and will have their health greatly impaired.

If you want to stay on top and prevent a stressful situation, know the risk factors involved with your life style. Carry out a life style that minimizes these risk factors. Good health to you!

The Need For Optimism

Optimism is a disposition or a tendency to look on the more favourable side of happenings or possibilities. Optimism also means that we believe that good ultimately predominates over evil in this world. Optimism is a noun. The verb for it is "to optimize." This verb speaks about action, action toward effective, perfect or useful activities to optimize whatever situation faces us. It is to obtain maximum efficiency.

We believe strongly in this trait of optimism. We believe it is at the core of the recovery process. What are we trying to say in this book? If we look at a number of troublesome mental and emotional disorders, we note that the problems are more severe and are made worse if an attitude of pessimism pervades. You and I know that it is hard to be optimistic all the time, especially when troubles surround us. But being optimistic is not sticking your head in the sand at all. Yes, we need to accept whatever troubles come our way and we need to face them and work through them. If we can hold an attitude towards optimism, believe in it, believe in ourselves and believe in goodness and expect the best we possibly can under those circumstances, we will have a much greater chance of success in health, happiness and in the quality of life.

There are certainly many problems in this world for which we could feel that it is proper and right to hold attitudes of pessimism. There are people who need to cope with setbacks or divorce and separation or with school problems. We are thinking also of families who have children with many disabilities or adults who suffer from all kinds of medical disabilities, or mental and emotional disorders. Problems abound in our world, but with optimism we can have an attitude that we "can beat this thing." There are things we can do to make the best of the situation and some good will come out of it and our health will be improved if we are optimistic. Although this strategy is not perfect, nor is it the only strategy that is possible, it will produce a better quality of living. You see, optimism is an attitude but it also has a biological root. The two are connected.

When our attitude becomes affected, so do the biological rhythms, the transmission of chemicals that influence our moods and our mind. So if we can hold an attitude of optimism, then life will clearly become easier for us because the body will respond to our optimism. First, to hold this positive attitude we need to view life as having its struggles and setbacks and expect this. We need to hold the attitude that we will do whatever we can to beat any trouble that comes along. It is an irrational belief that life will be without problems.

Second, most people do have setbacks but they realize that these setbacks are temporary. There is light at the end of the tunnel and we need to believe in it, we need to believe that things will get better. Thus, we need to look beyond the immediate and towards the future.

Third, we know it is often very difficult, but we need to look for the good even in all the negative things around us. Think about what is right and what is good, and what we have becomes worthy and worthwhile. We need to search for positives among the negatives.

Fourth, we need to take one step at a time and look for small changes and not big ones. When these small changes come, we need to say to ourself that this is good, that we expected it. Now let us try for another small change.

And fifth, when we are absolutely overcome with fear and doubt, we need to stop our mind from dwelling on these things. We have the control to stop these thoughts, to redirect our mind to other things. It will take energy. We can admit that we are afraid or angry and yet we can tell ourselves that this is enough. We will not take this anymore! We can make a step towards hope if we stop the negative thoughts. Consciously stop the mind from wandering to the negative.

Each day we should think of at least one positive thought or do one positive action. Think of this as success. Tomorrow we will find another positive thought or action. Use every available scrap of energy to find alternatives. Maybe these alternatives are not the ideal ones for which we had hoped, but let's take it one step at a time. And of course, we can always look to others for support, discussion or advice. Let us not be too shy nor too proud to seek out others with whom we can share our burdens.

Optimism is an attitude but it also is a **choice**. It is learned and not inherited, so we can change our feelings and our attitude towards optimism. Hope truly does spring eternal and is eternal. You and I have built-in resources, almost like a self-help therapist living inside. We have been given these resources, so let us use them. We need to learn how to tap into these resources. Maybe we need experts to help us tap into these resources. Either way we have them available. Let us use them for our benefit each day. This is a book about hope. We all have responsibility in masterminding our success. After all, if we do not do it, who will?

Chapter Three

STRESS MANAGEMENT STRATEGIES FOR STUDENTS

Our world is changing. It is estimated that children in elementary school will likely be involved in three to five different careers, rather than just one. With the 'knowledge explosion' it has become necessary for adults to 'retool' or become students again. Many retired individuals are back at school to pursue interests, postponed because of a hectic lifestyle . The strategies in this chapter are for all students of all ages because more and more of us will be needing them.

Revitalization Strategies

ADAPT *your priorities and expectations*
>   *each day plan what is most important to you
>   *make yourself your first priority
>   *accent the achievable

ATTEMPT *the realistic*
>   *have clear, simple and realistic expectations   for each day
>   *write them down
>   *scale down overambitious dreams and projects

ADJUST *your attitude*
>   *open up your outlook; take in new information
>   *decide to energize yourself
>   *relabel your experiences in a positive light

ATTACK *a new problem or challenge*

>   *change jobs/fields
>   *take on new projects
>   *volunteer for a new assignment
>   *write an article

ACT *out of caring and respect for you*

>   *reward and reinforce yourself and those around you
>   *say "no" sometimes, even if it feels uncomfortable
>   *assert your rights

ACCLAIM *your achievements and strengths*

>   *choose a "strength of the day" to focus on and enjoy
>   *keep a journal of your accomplishments
>   *brag about your day in minute detail to a caring companion
>   *acknowledge and savour compliments

ACKNOWLEDGE *your vulnerabilities*

>   *each day recognize a limitation
>   *commiserate with your colleagues
>   *talk about your feelings of helplessness

WORK *co-operatively*

>   *work with others on a project

When Writing A Test

1. **Survey the test.**
    *   * Determine relative difficulty of the items.
    *   * Determine how long you can take per item.
    *   * Conserve your time.
2. **Know the ground rules.**
    *   * Indicate your answers in the manner specified.
    *   * Understand the scoring rules.
3. **Relax - Do not Panic.**

4. **Answer items you know first!**
   Go back to the difficult ones **if** you have time.
   Set up a time schedule for completion.
5. **Read questions** and possible answers in their entirety.
6. **Do not change answers** unless you are sure.
   Changing answers based on "hunches" is poor procedure.
   Studies indicate a changed answer is wrong three out of four times
   unless one has recalled additional information.
7. **Work first and fast on items that yield the most points** in a given
   amount of time.
8. **Complete the statement before looking at the choices**, if the question is
   in the form of an incomplete statement.
9. **Analyze qualifiers** in the questions.
10. **Omit or guess** on items that stump you.
    (See 'guessing techniques').

Key Words (Qualifiers)

Try this and see if you can pick out the most important words.

Directions:- Identify and underline the qualifier(s) in the following:
1. Geniuses are usually queerer than people of average intelligence.
2. Only human beings, not animals, have the capacity to think.
3. Much of human behaviour is instinctive.
4. Slow learners remember what they learn better than fast learners.
5. Intelligent people form most of their opinions by logical reasoning.
6. A psychologist is a person who is trained to psychoanalyse people.
7. You can size up a person very well in an interview.
8. When one is working for several hours it is better to take a few long rests
   than several short ones.
9. The study of mathematics exercises the mind so that a person can think
   more logically in other subjects.
10. Grades in college have little to do with success in business careers.
11. Alcohol, taken in small amounts, is a stimulant.
12. There is a clear distinction between the normal person and one
    who is mentally ill.

13. Prejudices are mainly due to lack of information.
14. Competition among people is characteristic of most human societies.
15. The feature of a job that is most important to employees is the pay they get for their work.
16. It is possible to effectively classify people into introverts and extroverts.
17. Punishment is usually the best way to eliminate undesirable behaviour in children.
18. By closely watching a person's expression, you can readily tell the emotions that are being experienced.
19. The higher one sets his goals in life, the more he is sure to accomplish and the happier he will be.
20. If a person is honest with you, he usually can tell you what his motives are.

The key words for each question were as follows:
(1) usually, (2) only, not, (3) much, (4) better, (5) most, (6) psychoanalyse, (7) very well, (8) better, (9) in other subjects, (10) little, (11) stimulant, (12) clear, (13) mainly, (14) most, (15) most important, (16) effectively, (17) usually, best, (18) quite well, (19) sure, happier, (20) usually.
All the statements are false.

Guessing Techniques *(If guessing is not penalized.)*

1. Look for options that are ruled out on grammatical grounds.
2. When two choices begin with the same prefix or syllable, one of them is usually the correct choice.
3. Answers to some questions can be found in information given in other questions. (Read all items first.)
4. The more specific an answer is, the more likely it is to be correct.
5. The longer choice (largest number of words used) is a good bet in an emergency.
6. The correct choice usually is not the first or last option.
7. Logical Position: It will not be one of the extremes of a set of options which can be put in some natural order.
8. Similarity or oppositeness: It will usually be one of two similar statements or it will be one of two options which state the idea or fact diametrically opposite.

How to Take Notes

If you lack experience in taking lecture notes, you will probably find when going over your first efforts that you can not find the ideas for all the words.

Every word the lecturer says is not important, but the ideas are! You should try to put down on paper only short summary phrases of the main points of the lecture, which will recall the main ideas.

Here are a few more basic rules for making notes:

1. The lecture period should be spent mostly in listening for the main ideas, then writing down short summary phrases in your own words.

2. Most lecturers give only a few main points. Do not try to record every word the lecturer says-- you will get so snowed under with details, you will not remember the major theme.

3. Notice the cues the lecturer uses to highlight the main ideas of his discussion. Some of the most common cues are pauses, direct statements such as, "this is important," blackboard writing, outlines, lists of important points, summary statements, and phrases like "first. . ., second..., and lastly." Other cues may be changes in pace, volume, increased eye contact and repetition of specific points.

4. Use abbreviations in your note-making whenever possible - but be consistent.

5. A large sized notebook is best because it allows you to organize an entire unit on one page, with room to add information from reading assignments and to connect related ideas.

6. Lecture notes should be reviewed as soon as possible after they are taken, so you can fill in additional information you may remember and make sure the summaries you have written recall the original meaning. If you leave the notes overnight or longer without checking them, they may be completely useless in trying to recall what the lecturer said.

7. If you discover your notes are incomplete or leave you puzzled - do something about it. Ask your instructor to clear up the questions you have, discuss them with your classmates, or look for the answers in your textbooks.

The lecture situation is a common and significant aspect of student life. Students who feel that they can "cut" classes and/or take "a few notes in each class" will find themselves missing out on a very important part of their education. Break the note- taking process down into three parts: (1) before, (2) during, and (3) after the class.

Before: In order to be adequately prepared to take lecture notes, at least two criteria must be met. You must be prepared to receive information and you must have some format or approach for receiving. Concerning the former, read chapters and articles related to each day's lecture before coming to the class and review your previous notes prior to the class.

Having a format or approach that will best allow you to take good notes means that both the notebook itself and the organization of it must be effective and efficient for you.

Good advice is that you purchase a sturdy, three-ring, loose-leaf notebook, one that can be fitted with tabular dividers. Once it is purchased, try these suggestions:

- Keep all notes and hand-outs for each of your classes in separate sections.
- Start your notes for a new chapter on a new page.
- Start your notes for a new lecture on a new page
  ("lecture" does not always equal one class hour - a lecture is a topic that corresponds, more or less, to a chapter in the book).
- Label each set of notes (date and brief statement of topic).
- Keep all notes in your notebook.

During: You have made a sound investment.
Make it work for you. Attend all lectures and use a note-taking format that is effective for **you**. We suggest the following:
Get there early. . .
1. Sit up front.
2. Review your notes.
Become actively involved. . .
1. Use your eyes, ears and mouth to take notes.
2. Prepare to concentrate as completely as possible.
3. **Listen** to the **lecturer**--do not concentrate on voice or mannerisms.
Take good notes. . .
1. Use an outline format.
2. Copy everything from the board, not everything that is said.

After: Assuming that you have taken the advice offered above, you are at least half-way there in terms of understanding and retaining information from lectures. Your next step is to review your class and textbook notes at regular intervals.

Students usually find that a quick review of class notes immediately after each session and another review immediately preceding each session is very valuable.

Cornell Method - Five R's of Note Taking

Record:
Lecture notes in the 6" column.

Reduce:
As soon as possible, summarize ideas and facts concisely in the 2" column.

Recite:
Cover the 6" column using only the jottings in the 2" columns as cues or 'flags' to help you recall. Then, uncovering the notes, verify what you have said.

Reflect:
Think! Develop personal analogies, ideas and relationships
(record at the bottom of page).

Review:
Repeat step 3 every week or so.
Space for analogies, ideas and relationships.

```
|---------2"----|-------------------------------6"----------------|

REDUCE NOTES                    NOTES

—————————— A)    ————————————————————

—————————— B)    ————————————————————
                 ————————————————————

                 1. ————————————————————
                 2. ————————————————————
                 3. ————————————————————
```

Two purposes: *Clarification of concepts*
                         Preparation for essay exams

MORE SUGGESTIONS ON NOTE TAKING

BASIC DOS

Take notes at every lecture. The instructor has something to say which you will need to know to pass the tests. You will need notes to help you remember what was important that day.

Mark the day and date on each set of notes (e.g. Monday, Oct. 24). This helps if you are absent, making it easy for you to locate the "empty spot" in your notes and either ask the instructor in his office about that lecture or borrow notes from a good student in your class.

Develop your own "shorthand" to make note-taking easier. For example, you might use **&** for and, **w/** for with, **w/o** for without, etc.

Organize your day's notes into divisions as you take them. For example, use Roman numeral I for the first main idea, with A, B, C, etc. under I for characteristics, evidence, or examples of the main idea or principle. When the instructor begins to discuss the next main idea, change to Roman numeral II with A's and B's, etc. under that for the related supporting material.

End the day's notes with a restatement or summary in your own words of what that day's lecture was mainly about. Be sure you could answer the question, "What did he discuss today?" or "What did all those examples prove?"

Include charts, drawings or illustrations on the board in your notes. Often, they make clear or sum up what is said in a lecture.

Look up big or unfamiliar words the instructor uses in class when you get home. Write the definitions on the same page as the word(s) appear in your notes.

Try to have a kind of silent conversation with the lecturer as he talks. When he makes a statement, silently ask, "Why?" Perhaps his next sentence will begin to answer your question.

Underline or write in capital letters things which you know the lecturer is emphasizing. If she likes dates, record and underline them. If he likes examples, record and star them. If she likes general rules or principles, underline those. (Do not waste time emphasizing things which the professor does not consider important!)

Rewrite your notes as a study guide. It is helpful to look back over the notes as soon after class as possible to review and "nail down" the information in your head. (To review for a test, it is often useful to rewrite - even in a shortened form - your notes. This helps you remember the material when you begin writing the test.)

BASIC DON'TS

Miss class. You can not get the benefit of the lecture if you are not there.

Be late to class. The teacher usually begins his lecture with the main idea he is going to discuss, for part or all of that class period. If you are even five minutes late, you may miss the main idea and not know what the lecture is about until the very end.

Write constantly. It interferes with your listening. Only write when the instructor states a main idea, gives evidence or examples, or sums up.

Try to write everything the instructor says. Notes that tell "everything" do not tell anything about what was most important or what was only an example or even a joke.

Write long, complicated sentences. These are too hard to review for tests. You might as well have to re-read the whole textbook assignments as to try to read long, boring notes.

Separate main ideas or principles from their evidence or examples. Keep all the material which is closely related written in the same part of your notes. (Perhaps you could skip lines between the lines you write in case you need to go back and add an example related to an earlier statement.)

Repeat the same idea or phrase over and over in one set of lecture notes. Perhaps you could underline or star an important phrase or idea every time the instructor repeats it.

Tune out the instructor! You must keep listening, even when you are not interested or sure of what her point is. She is getting to her point all the time, and the part you tune out may be the most important or a vital step in the total process she's describing.

Change the instructor's words too much when you put them in your notes. Each discipline (area of study) has a vocabulary of its own, and one way to learn it is to write it in your notes.

Leave the class confused, if you can help it! Ask questions at an appropriate point in the lecture period, or see the professor at the end of class to ask about any part of the lecture which has confused you.

Motivation and You in College

There are three major ingredients to success in college:

1. **Basic Intelligence:** This is rarely enough by itself. Good grades in high school are no guarantee of good grades in college.

2. **Ability To Work Constructively: "Working constructively" is different than "working hard."** Effective study habits can be learned and made habitual and often make the difference between passing and failing grades.

3. **Will To Succeed:** The major difference between success and failure in college is a well-defined and realistic goal.

It is nearly impossible to work constructively without a goal. If you can establish goals, even temporary or provisional ones, your motivation to attain these goals will encourage you to gain the skills essential to success in college. You can set up goals by evaluating yourself, your needs, interests and aptitudes.

Establishing goals today does not have to mean a final commitment, but it can provide you with direction and impetus (motivation) for achievement.

1. The primary cause of flunking out is **NOT** lack of ability but is usually unwillingness of the student **to learn how to study effectively.**

2. Your attitudes toward success are of crucial importance in matters like survival in college and completion of a degree program. These attitudes will depend upon what success means to you. Ask yourself what success is for you: a comfortable life? an opportunity to serve others? a chance to be creative? In other words, is a college career something you require in order to meet your own personal needs for success?

3. You can be taught techniques of effective study, but the effort, time and self-discipline to make them work can only be provided by **YOU.**

R E M E M B E R !

Study Skills

Reading and Remembering Guide - SQ3R

Many college freshmen find reading assignments to be the most difficult to handle. Educators have devised a simple, five-step system for developing higher level study skills that promotes faster and more meaningful reading, makes it easier to prepare for quizzes and results in appreciably higher course grades. The system is called the **Survey Q3R Method.**

1. **SURVEY** the reading assignment quickly, taking no more than five minutes to glance over the whole assignment.
    READ the **introductory and summary paragraphs,** inspect all **illustrations and tables** check the **heading and subheadings.** They will reveal the important points to be presented and indicate how these points are related.

2. **CLOSE** the book and ask yourself the following **QUESTION: "What are the main points** that the author is trying to tell me?" Early identification of these will aid you in preparing for later examinations.

3.   **READ** the assignment carefully for meaning. When you read, do not read passively as you would an adventure story. Such novels are for entertainment and are written without any concern for whether or not you remember detail. Read actively!
   * make questions out of the topic sentences of paragraphs and look for the answers as you read
   * **underline key words and phrases** to aid you in recalling the main outline of the chapter
   * **summarize key points in your own words** in the page margin of the book.

4.   **STOP** at intervals and **RECITE** to yourself from memory **the main points** of the assignment, recalling only the essential details to understand what the author is trying to say.

5.   **REVIEW** the assignment at **periodic intervals** to refresh your memory and make the facts stick. Do not wait until just before the examination to do your reviewing. That's a good time for the final review, but not for the first review.

How To Retain Information

Rapid forgetting seems to plague almost everyone. There are, however, a few simple rules which you may follow to help retard forgetting.

1.   **Understand the material** you are studying.
   Material which is meaningful to you will be better remembered than things which are unclear.

2.   **Study frequently** in short periods rather than trying to learn everything all at once.

3.   **Restate key points** in your own words. Write them out or say them to yourself or to a friend. You will be required to do this on examinations and you might as well learn how to express important concepts in your own words right from the start. Also, expressing the main points in your own words will make it much easier to remember them later.

4. **Learn to use memory cues.** Develop a system for employing key words and symbols to remind you of important details. When reading a textbook, try to find a key word or two which symbolizes for you the main point in each paragraph.

    Pay particular attention to:

    a) **subheadings**

    b) **first and last sentences** in paragraphs

    c) **tables, figures and diagrams**

    By memorizing a few key words and symbols it is possible to reconstruct all the major ideas in the chapter.

5. **Practice using the Survey Q3R Method** until it seems the natural way to study your reading assignments.

How to Increase Reading Speed

1. **Do not whisper the words as you read, or form them with your lips or tongue.** Do not point them out to yourself. All this slows up your reading.

2. **Do not let yourself regress**. If you have a habit of going back and rereading phrases or sentences, force yourself to go on. Do not let yourself reread them.

3. You do not have to strain your eyes, mind, or muscles in order to read fast. **Relax**--let the print flow into your mind through your eyes, instead of feverishly chasing the words with your mind.

4. **Try to see phrases, sentences and even whole paragraphs at a glance**, and grab their central meaning with one clutch of the mind's fingers. Do not stop on particular words (but if you feel it is an important word, take the trouble to look up in a dictionary any word you do not understand). Make the eye movement a steadily forward one.

5. **If you find your mind wandering as you read, do not become impatient;** do not fight it--simply make a mental or written note to take up that problem when you get around to it. Actually writing a memo will often push the intruding idea out of the mind until the reading session is finished.

6. The most important rule is to **try to think out in advance what the author is going to say.** Do not simply blot up ideas. Keep your curiosity alive, and keep up your interest in what you are reading by asking yourself whether the author is developing an idea as you would expect it to develop it if you were doing the writing.

7. **Be flexible**. You should not have a single speed but several different speeds. You should shift from one speed to another in view of: your **purpose** in reading the material, the **difficulty** of the material and your own personal **familiarity** with the subject matter. Your goal, then, is not rapid reading in every situation, but a flexible rate which you will adjust to the demands of every reading task. It is seldom necessary to read every word of every sentence.

    *This is an adaptation of the Watson-Newcomb Rules by the New York Daily News.

How to Answer Essay Questions

1. Read all essay items, noting beside each question the points that occur to you.

2. Organize your answer before writing. (Outline)

3. Write to the point-if you know your stuff.

4. Write something for every question, even if you do not know your stuff.

5. Answer in outline form if time does not permit a complete essay answer.

6. Write legibly.

How to Answer Sentence Completion Items

1. Guess, even if you are not sure of the answer (partial credit may be awarded).

2. Make the completed statement logically consistent.

3. Make use of grammar to help decide the correct answer:
   a) **an** before the blank means the answer begins with a vowel.
   b) **a** before the blank means the answer begins with a consonant.
   c) use of certain modifiers in the sentence may indicate the degree of generality desired in the answers.
   Example:
   > The plans for the invasion of Germany during World War II were devised by the _____.
   > The answer is "General staff."
   > The (the) before General rules out the name of a person.

4. Consider the number and length of the blanks to be completed.

How to Write an Essay Exam

1. Notice carefully the directive **verb** that tells you what you should do in your answer. Directive verbs that are commonly used in examinations are: explain, enumerate, list, name, justify, defend, account for, sketch, clarify, state, illustrate and discuss.

2. Outline and preplan your answer if it is to be any length at all. For this purpose, use scratch paper or the back of the examination paper. Preplanning will help you to write an organized instead of haphazard answer.

3. Stick to the question. Give the information you have that is directly relevant to the question and present it in an orderly way. Resist the temptation to write about something you know more about instead.

4. Begin your answer with a general statement or topic sentence.

5. Read directions carefully. Ask the instructor questions if you do not fully understand them.

6. Read **all** questions carefully before answering any of them, and make sure you clearly understand each question. Note key words such as "name," "describe," "explain," "compare," etc.

7. If you have a choice as to which questions to answer, make up your mind quickly.

8.   Make a quick allotment of time for each question so that you will not be caught short on the last question. If the point value for the questions is weighted, plan your time accordingly.

9.   Answer the easiest first.

10. **Before** you begin writing, prepare a short outline of the main points you intend to cover. Spend some time organizing your material.

11. Organize your answer in three parts:
     a) Introduction. **SAY WHAT YOU ARE GOING TO SAY.**
     b) Main Body. **SAY IT.**
     c) Summary. **SAY WHAT YOU JUST SAID.**

12. Make your papers neat; write legibly.

13. Do not leave a question blank if you are unsure of your answer. Instructors are bound to give you some credit for trying.

14. Save a few minutes for proofreading.

Key Instructional Words in Essay Exams

COMPARE

When you are asked to **compare**, you should examine qualities or characteristics in order to discover resemblances. The term **compare** is usually stated as **compare with**, and it implies that you are to emphasize similarities, although differences may be mentioned.

CONTRAST

When you are instructed to contrast, dissimilarities, differences or unlikenesses of associated things, qualities, events or problems should be stressed.

CRITICIZE

In a criticism you should express your judgement with respect to the correctness or merit of the factors under consideration. You are expected to give the results of your own analysis and to discuss the limitations and good points or contributions of the plan or work in question.

DEFINE

Definitions call for concise, clear and authoritative meanings. In such statements details are not required but boundaries or limitations of the definitions should be briefly cited. You must keep in mind the class to which a thing belongs and whatever differentiates that particular object from all others in the class.

DESCRIBE

In a descriptive answer you should recount, characterize, sketch or relate in narrative form.

DIAGRAM

For a question which specifies a diagram, you should present a drawing, chart, plan, or graphic representation in your answer. Generally, the student is also expected to label the diagram and in some cases to add a brief explanation or description.

DISCUSS

The term **discuss**, which appears often in essay questions, directs you to examine, analyze carefully and present considerations (pro and con) regarding the problems or items involved. This type of question calls for a complete and detailed answer.

ENUMERATE

The word **enumerate** specifies a list or outline form of reply. In such questions you should recount, one by one, in concise form the points required.

EVALUATE

In an evaluation you are expected to present a careful appraisal of the problem, stressing both advantages and limitations. Evaluation implies authoritative and, to a lesser degree, personal appraisal of both contributions and limitations.

EXPLAIN

In explanatory answers it is imperative that you clarify, elucidate and interpret the material you present. In such an answer it is best to state the "how" and "why," reconcile any differences in opinion or experimental results and, where possible, state causes. The aim is to make plain the conditions which give rise to whatever you are examining.

ILLUSTRATE

A question which asks you to illustrate usually requires explanation. You are expected to translate, exemplify, solve or comment upon the subject and usually to give your judgment or reaction to the problem.

INTERPRET

An interpretation question is similar to one requiring explanation. You are expected to translate, exemplify, solve or comment upon the subject and usually to give your judgement or reaction to the problem.

JUSTIFY

When you are instructed to justify your answer, you must prove or show grounds for decisions. In such an answer, evidence should be presented in convincing form.

LIST

Listing is similar to enumeration. You are expected in such questions to present an itemized series or a tabulation. Such questions should always be given in concise form.

OUTLINE

An outlined answer is organized description. You should give main points and essential supplementary materials, omitting minor details and presenting the information in a systematic arrangement or classification.

PROVE

A question which requires proof is one which demands confirmation or verification. In such discussions you should establish something with certainty by evaluating and citing experimental evidence or by logical reasoning.

RELATE

In a question which asks you to show the relationship or to relate, your answer should emphasize connections and association in descriptive form.

Improving Your Child's School Performance

Our children's education is important. There are things that we can do as parents to ensure our children's success during these vital years.

1. *Insist upon regular attendance.*

   Irregular or sporadic attendance can become habitual. Perhaps the main responsibility of parents with respect to a child's schooling is to make sure the child is in attendance. "You can't succeed if you don't try."

2. *Focus on positives.*

   Every time a child brings an assignment home, there will be an opportunity for the parent to focus on a positive or a negative feature. For example, if a child spells seventeen words correctly out of twenty, my suggestion would be to focus on what is correct and then suggest the child can do even better.Constant focus on mistakes can create the impression that the child is always failing.

3. *Spend time on school activities.*

   Most parents with younger children do discuss school activities almost every day. This is exceptionally valuable but should not stop as the child proceeds through the grades. Show an interest in your child. If the child is to perceive school as being important, then it must be talked about and discussed at home, at the same level as parental activities.

4. *Engender close communication and cooperation with the school.*

   Sometimes parents may wish to be critical of a teacher, a school or a school system. This is not necessarily harmful, but the strategy for the child is that the school and home are working together to provide the best education possible. Find out about your child's strengths and weaknesses, keep in touch, become involved in parent teacher associations and help out when needed.

5. *Emphasize the importance of academic pursuits in your own lifestyle.*

   Children model their parents. If there are books in the home, if reading is seen to be important, then children will want to learn to read. It's that simple. If in daily discussions parents place a high value on education, then children will see education to be important. Telling a child to work hard in school when there does not appear as any connection with home activities creates confusion, rather than a good mind set for academic excellence.

6.   *Reward efforts and performance in homework.*

So often parents insist the children spend "X" number of minutes per night on homework. I would discourage this practice and replace it with finding out what homework your child has to do, allowing the child to take the necessary time to complete the assignment and then rewarding both the child's effort and performance. Time itself is not nearly as important a factor as the effort, enthusiasm and work strategies that the child employs.

7.   *Make use of special services offered by your school district.*

Many school districts employ specialists such as speech clinicians, reading specialists, school psychologists, elementary counsellors, etc. If you keep abreast of these services in school, you will then be in a position to ask for these specialized personnel when they are needed. The more we know about our child's abilities, work habits, strengths and weaknesses, the better able we are to assist with decision-making and keeping realistic expectations as part of our family discussions.

8.   *Be alert to spot areas of strength and talent.*

We often think of providing extra tutoring in areas of weakness, however, it is just as important for parents to know about subjects our child really enjoys and excels in. Often the best way to improve attitudes towards education is to encourage children to be involved in school and extracurricular activities in areas where they perform well. Look for strengths. Hockey coaches do not put a slow, strong defenceman on the forward line. The coach goes with the players strengths which leads to success and self-esteem. We feel good when we things well and when we feel we are successful.

In the past we have given seminars and lectures to students as well as teachers. This next section is helpful not only to teachers, but also to parents who are interested in knowing the procedures followed by the school when your child is experiencing difficulty. If you are concerned and feel that your child may be depressed, you should contact the school and discuss these suggestions.

A Teacher's Guide To Treating Children's Depression

1. In the classroom, seat the depressed and unhappy child near the teacher and make a special effort to involve the child in class activities. Have the child assume specific tasks like passing out papers or being a helper in some other way, to keep the child alert and interested. Keep the child too busy to brood.

2. Encourage the parents to explore the possibility of medication and to talk to the family doctor. Seek the causes of the depression: death in the family, bitter disappointment, repressed hostility?

3. Such a child should be referred immediately to a local mental health centre. The child will not likely perform effectively in the classroom due to emotional problems and little improvement will occur until these problems are resolved. This child will not do well on time-tasks in school. Breaking up long assignments into small segments may be beneficial. Continued pressure will be detrimental; omit home tutoring. A warm, supporting teacher-pupil relationship is essential.

4. Obtain behaviour therapy for the child. Utilize assertive training to help the child control more areas of life. Also, reinforce consistently and heavily all spontaneous or requested behaviours involving activity, work, action, play, movement, conversation, projects, discussion and participation. Offer tokens for any variety of actions taken to be traded for money or desired possessions or privileges. The child should have obligations and responsibilities to groups and parents. Interrupt the child's depression with instruction, demands and assignments, and set time limits for completion of work.

5. Seek the source of the child's bodily complaints. The child may have an ulcer. The stomach ache may be derived from test anxiety and fear of failure. Place the child in a less demanding curriculum even if they are bright, as they obviously cannot tolerate the stress.

6.   For a child with migraine headaches, relieve the tension from the child's daily routine. Reduce all sources of perfectionistic standards. Give the child more freedom to express their own ideas among siblings and/or classmates.

7.   Discuss with the parents critical medical and psychological aspects of this behaviour and refer the child for psychiatric help, assuring the parents of the need and then working with them until the child is in treatment. Attempt to alleviate the causes where known, and to lessen the problem until therapy begins.

8.   Children should not receive any secondary gain from their symptoms if this pattern is to diminish. Requests to go to the school nurse should be evaluated carefully, and pampering should be minimized. However, the teacher should be supportive and give children the opportunity to talk about what is upsetting them.

9.   Students have considerable anxiety caused by academic and parental pressures. The social and emotional pressures are frequently caused by a demanding parent. This parent should focus on the child's health and adjustment rather than on grades or the ambitions of the parent. Family therapy is recommended.

10. Bibliotherapy is often most effective in dealing with transient emotional problems. There exists a wealth of books related to well-known problems experienced by many children. For example, if a child is concerned about his small physical stature, a newly born sibling or being adopted, the teacher can encourage the child to read about it. If, on the other hand, there is interest in sexual reproduction, masturbation, pregnancy or birth control, then the first step is to have correct information to dispel myths and ignorance.

11. An especially sensitive teacher may develop a mental health unit in class which deals with people's feelings. This unit might emphasize particularly the emotion with which the troubled child is having difficulty. She should encourage all the children's verbalizations about their feelings. Perhaps the teacher or the children might invite the school psychologist into the classroom to talk about people's feelings and the reasons for them.

12. For feelings of inferiority in a child:
    DO Inspire confidence in the child's ability.
    DO Supply work to help the child "catch up" with the group.
    DO Test specific areas of achievement and devise a program at these levels.
    DO Capitalize on strengths shown by tests and interviews.
    DO Let the child do something to help in the classroom.
    DO Express appreciation for effort.
    DO Appoint the child to "head" a committee.
    DO Include the child in a spirited special panel on "emotionally charged"
        topics such as crime and pollution.
    DO Include the child in a group whose work merits special recognition.
    DO Send a note home telling of good effort.
    DO Involve the child in class discussion, questions and activities.
    DO Make observation projects involving social behaviour in the cafeteria,
        halls, downtown and theatres. Teach these children to watch for
        desirable and undesirable behaviour in others.

13. Some children feel inferior or behave badly or ineffectively in physical education
    and art classes and similar areas because of lack of coordination or feelings of
    shame. For example, in gym some children may be embarrassed because of their
    size, weight or general ineptitude. Give some special "tutoring" in how to shoot a
    basket or perform some tumbling activity; the child may develop more confidence.
    Many children dislike these special areas, not because they cannot do well in some
    aspect of the program, but because they fear ridicule, may it be real or imagined.
    Such children might be asked to help score or keep time until developing some skill
    in the activity.

    We have given you stress management techniques on both short and long-term bases
and also strategies to help the student. It may be necessary to go back and look at these things
one more time. We suggest that you try the short-term strategies immediately, especially
exercise, diet and relaxation. If worry is a problem for you, go back and look at how you can control
it. If you have a particular problem area right now that needs some emotional release, try our
short-term ideas. As you plan your next weekend trip take the book along and look at the long-
term coping action plan and work it through with the significant other in your life. Try to look for
the positives, the silver lining, the sun shining brightly above. Tell yourself to think of the positives
and, in the meantime, you are actively planning long-term strategies.

Chapter Four

STRESS MANAGEMENT
IN THE WORKPLACE

The Social Context of the Workplace in Canada

We begin this chapter with a few facts that are taken from Statistics Canada to help us understand the nature of the work setting and the factors that are involved in understanding the stressors in the workplace. We want to state at the outset that we recognize fully that women who are full-time homemakers are considered by us to also have a workplace, namely, in the home. Our statistics will show the nature of the changing social context within which people must find effective employment and within which they must work and survive.

The annual growth rate in Canada in terms of population is set at 1.4% with immigration rates of 199,140 people per year accounting for the bulk of the increase. This statistic shows us that we cannot argue that it is the immigrants that are taking away the few available jobs. Statistics show that the immigrants that are allowed into Canada have a higher education and are more eligible for the white collar jobs. However, immigration rates are not consistently high in Canada. The median income for a family in Canada is set at $44,460.00. The median represents that figure at which 50% of the population are above that income and 50% are below. Of those below that figure, 9.6% of the population have a low income, that is, an income below $24,000.00 per year, an income deemed to be at the poverty level in this country. The other interesting fact is that women earn 65.8% of men's salaries in equivalent jobs. Clearly, there is a frustration on the part of women in the work force because it is quite evident that women do not get paid as much as men do for the same job. The birth rate is declining and is currently set at 15.0 per one thousand and the divorce rate at 3.1 per one thousand people in Canada. Divorce rates have steadily increased and are highest in Western Canada, estimated at somewhere between 43 to 47%. While fewer children are being born and thus looking for work in the future, a greater number of families are being split up through divorce, hence increasing the number of women in the work force. Indeed, women's participation in the work force is steadily increasing and in 1992 it was set at 58.4%. Of the approximately 12,572,000 people employed in Canada in 1993, 58.4% of these are unionized. We mention the union factor because it often sets up many stress conditions with labour fighting management and vice versa. The current unemployment rate is set at 8.1% in Canada with certain provinces having a higher rate. The province of Alberta, for example, has an unemployment rate of 9.4%.

In Canada there are 5,151,800 children in elementary and secondary schools, plus 865,300 students in full-time post-secondary enrolment. Government expenditure on education is 5.6% of the Gross National Product and yet Canada spends 25.9% of the GNP on social programs and only 5.9% on health. The annual inflation rate as of 1992 was estimated at 4.8%. While we had a good number of our children in school, public school enrolment declined during the first half of the 1980's but there was an upward trend in the early part of the 1990's. The fact is that students are dropping out of school at an alarming rate. Estimates vary by province and school districts but they run as high as 25% in some areas, with the bulk of students dropping out in grades 10, 11 and 12. Thus, we have more young people looking for work than ever before, young people who have little or no experience with how to operate in the workplace.

Another factor that we encounter in the workplace is the ability of Canadians to conduct conversations in both French and English. Many jobs now require this capability. Statistics Canada sets the figure at 16% as to the total number of people in the work force that can hold a conversation in both English and French, but that is up from 12% in 1961. In Quebec, 35% of the people are bilingual, and only 3% in Newfoundland and 5% in Saskatchewan are bilingual. Alberta's bilingualism rate currently is set at roughly 10 to 12%.

We must also consider as a factor the nature of child-care arrangements and the number of children requiring it since both parents are working out of the home. In 1990 there were 1.3 million preschoolers (under age six) and 1.7 million school-aged children (aged six to twelve) whose mothers were in the labour force. As many as three million children are in need of alternate child-care arrangements, up from 1.4 million in 1971. The continuing movement of women into the labour force and an increase in single-parent families will provide a demand for a variety of child-care forms. What we have seen in the last 20 years in this country is a tremendous awareness of the problems of latch-key children. These are children who come home from school with the house key dangling around their neck and nobody home to supervise them. This has caused increasing stress in the workplace since it turns out that parents need to be responsible for these children in some way. They sit at work worrying about what their children are doing, or make frequent phone calls to make sure that they are all right.

To help set the scene with respect to the social context of the workplace in Canada, another factor must be mentioned. Many individuals are in a middle-management position at work. This is a rather difficult place to work because you are responsible for employees working for you and yet you must report to a higher authority. In fact, middle-managers have the most difficult of all jobs because they have little authority but plenty of responsibility. Our recent research indicates that middle-managers are under far greater stress than the average employee who is not in a management position or the executive who has some power and authority to affect change. Governments are the greatest employers of middle-managers. Today, there are more women in middle-management positions than ever before. The increasing stress for them is that they also report having major responsibilities the home and children while being in a very responsible position at work with little authority to affect changes.

The above statistics can be found in a publication called Canadian Social Trends. This publication is available from Statistics Canada at a modest rate. We suggest that people should avail themselves of the opportunity of looking at all the facts and figures that Statistics Canada compiles to become more aware of the specific nature of factors determining social and political changes in the workplace in Canada. In any work setting we need to see more clearly what the various forces are that cause stress so as to be able to do something about it. This story illustrates what we are trying to say more clearly:

■■

One day, in the country, a man stopped to pass the time with a farmer who was reflectively surveying his fields. Our friend said, "There seems to be more rabbits about these days." The farmer's reply was, "Ah, yes, there are more rabbits because there is less disease and we have had good weather for the grass. Last year there was a lot of fox hunting and so now there are fewer predators. But they have stopped hunting the foxes this year because some of the hounds died, and there are more weasels this year and we have started shooting rabbits to eat, so next year there won't be so many rabbits." Our friend took a deep breath and said, "Say that again slowly, please."

This story illustrates that there are both resisting forces and pro-active forces that are involved in any stress situation or indeed in any business situation. Population of the rabbit now was caused by conditions such as good weather for grass, fewer rabbits shot, fewer foxes and less disease. On the other hand, resisting forces against the rabbit population were that there could be more foxes to hunt rabbits, more rabbits hunted by man and more weasels to eat the rabbits. We tell this story at our sessions to indicate that we must carefully look at all the forces for and against something in order to reduce stress and improve chances for success. When forces working for change and forces working against change are analyzed, diagrammed, detailed and discussed we have a better chance of surviving the 1990's and beyond.

The Parental Value-Shift and its Effect on the Workplace and the Home

Research clearly shows a tremendous value-shift today. To what extent this accounts for the problems in the workplace or in the home is still to be known, but we think that it has something to do with it. Parents will readily agree that today's children do not accept authority as they used to. We, as parents, may complain about it but we are the ones who have shifted our values: we want our children to think for themselves, accept responsibility, show initiative and be tolerant of opposing views. Either we accept the challenge given to us by our children or we shift our values back to traditional ones. Which do we want? This value-shift has had far-reaching consequences. Teachers have had trouble disciplining children in the schools either because we disagree with their methods or we do not openly support or reinforce their efforts in the classroom. Our children have been raised to show open challenge to schools, courts, laws, church leaders, political leaders and business organizations. Our children have learned to challenge authority - beginning with our own authority. As we, in our society, have moved from demanding strict unquestioning discipline to child independence and initiative, we have inherited new challenges to successful integration in the workplace and to effective child discipline in the home.

There was a time in the 1950's, perhaps you remember it, when we gave great respect to church leaders, teachers, policemen and leaders in our business community. Children were raised to respect strict authority. Women did not wear pants nor did men wear earrings. Many of us grew up sitting on different sides of the church: men on one side and women on the other. God and church were respected. There was a time when we could drop in and visit friends without phoning ahead or making appointments. These changes have been quite evident through research surveys. During the 1950's loyalty to church, strict obedience, good manners and conduct and proper dress were valued by most people. All of these beliefs are linked to the value of conformity and upholding the letter of the law. By 1990 things have changed. While the push for the "me generation" began in 1975 and beyond, virtually opposite attitudes are now in the workplace. Our push for independence and autonomy has caused increasing concern with regards to loyalty to leaders whether in church, school or business. Obedience and good manners have given way to independence and egotism. These changes in traditional values that we see today sweep across all class lines and all employment situations.

You may ask, "Why the change?" Alvin Toffler, the futurist, suggested that these changes occurred because we live in an increasingly complex world. Parents wanted their children to succeed, to survive. They knew that good jobs required judgement and the ability for people to think for themselves. Increased technology demanded increased education and with it came a greater value for independence and intolerance of being told what to do. Toffler also suggests that the move away from an agricultural society has increased the demand for employment in the towns and cities. Increased urbanization brought with it many other problems such as crime, drugs, higher unemployment rates, greater poverty and increasing demands for education, health and welfare benefits.

Increasing education levels of our children and parents has also changed our values to some degree. Today, more than ever, we have a highly educated class of people in Canada, people who are well-read and have the ability to think and reason for themselves. So today employers are looking for people who believe in knowledge and can make decisions for themselves. Thus, we have begun to value knowledge and to teach it to our children.

The increasing number of mothers working out of the home meant that our children needed to be more self-reliant. Pressed for time and energy, parents have forced their children to become independent, doing much of what needs to be done for homework, meals and cleaning on their own. While this is not necessarily bad, it has moved our value system toward greater autonomy and independence and made it more difficult for some people to adjust to the work setting where there is a distinct hierarchy and line of authority.

And then one also needs to look at changes in religious attitude that have created this value shift. Some people still believe in obedience to church and God but that percentage in Canada is decreasing. Statistics Canada has shown that church attendance and belief in a higher authority have dramatically declined since 1948. In the 1960's, the second Vatican Council also helped shift values by breaking old rules and changing its views with respect to divorce and remarriage.

Thus, we are becoming increasingly more secular, increasing the pace of change with no common belief system. This is all too evident in the work setting, a place where we mingle and visit, work and play. No more do we have the reliance on the work setting for our social support system since people are so different today in what they believe and how they act. Not only do we differ from each other because of value-shifts, we differ through the impact of immigration. It is not unusual to be at a meeting of twelve people where each person is from or has roots in a different country. Given this situation we are caught in a struggle that has increased our stress. So the race is on and so is the stress. As the pressures of work and living pile up, we store up the stressors and over time begin to feel them take their toll on our health, relationships and work productivity. Our work takes up the majority of our energy and time because without it we cannot survive. Our experiences at work can often cause us to feel bitter, rejected, neglected and unloved. Many people respond by retreating further into themselves and shoring up their defences for protection. All our needs and desires, shaped by shifting values and painful experiences, have made it more difficult for us to establish new and meaningful relationships within and outside the work setting.

This chapter may be more important to us than any other because of our common experience of stressors at work. In the following pages we want to make a number of suggestions that you may find helpful in stress management in the workplace.

Major Stressors in the Workplace

We have spent a considerable number of years consulting a wide variety of businesses and agencies. We have also had a number of our graduate students, both at the masters and doctoral level, do research with respect to stress in the workplace. We recognize that work settings are very different. A number of books have been written on the stress faced by teachers and the stress of being an air traffic controller. We know that there are stressors unique to certain occupations and settings; however, we feel that there are some factors that are common to all settings that present work-related stress. The following is a list of 20 items that will summarize the major work-related stress factors:

1. Lack of support from administrators and superiors.
2. Having to meet too many deadlines.
3. Too much competitiveness.
4. Unfriendly collegial working atmosphere.
5. Interruptions during work.
6. Lack of promotion policies and opportunities.
7. Lack of job security.
8. Lack of job benefits including health, pension and social assistance.
9. Lack of recognition for work well done.
10. Inappropriate rewards for work well done.
11. Too much paper work.
12. Lack of input on evaluations.
13. Lack of opportunity to socialize with workpeers.
14. Working with a difficult boss.
15. Limited career advancement opportunities.
16. No support for stressors from home and family.
17. Inadequate facilities such as lighting and noise control.
18. Too many extra assignments.
19. Public criticisms on a private work matter.
20. Inability to resolve the demands of the job with other family duties.

While these factors are certainly not the only ones, they summarize the major work stressors that need to be recognized. Stress in the workplace is a combination of our personality, the nature of the job, the organization of the business and many other factors. However, most of the time it is true to say that when the stress we feel at home is brought to work, it will only increase the focus of the stress points on the job. I do not think that we could find anyone that could separate the home life from the work situation. However, there are certain things we can do at our job regardless of where the stress comes from. The suggestions that we will make at this present time are different from those in chapter two. However, we feel that they are specific to work- related stress and therefore need to be emphasized. Have a look at the 15 suggestions below.

▼ Success with Stress at Work

▼ *Don't Skate, Relate*
Build up your resources by being open and friendly. Sharing your troubles allows
▼ others to help.

▼ *Yielding at Times*
Don't stand your ground all the time, even in situations where you are dead certain
the other person is wrong. This builds relationships.
▼

Avoid Perfection
▼ A little bit of perfectionism is good, but expecting too much of self and others brings
constant arrogance. Others like people who screw up at times.

▼

Praise Others
▼ We have to have a bit of the competitive edge. Giving others words of praise really
helps you with your stress. It comes back to you four-fold.

▼ *Be Organized*
Time pressures frequently cause stress at work. Have a detailed time management
▼ plan for every day.

▼ *Be a Team Player*
You gain friends, recognition and support by mingling and joining in. "Looking out
for number 1" just increases stress at work.
▼

Try to be Flexible
▼ While we all have our specific roles and duties, being willing to help others at times
will cause others to help you when you need it.

▼

Avoid the Politics
Impossible to do at times, but try to remain neutral. Don't get caught up with
▼ political games, unless you want more stress.

Two Minute Relaxer
This is particularly important for people working at screens and typewriters. Close your eyes, breathe deeply and slowly and let your mind wander to a favourite spot for 2 minutes. Do this every hour.

Don't Procrastinate
Work will just pile up. Daily time- management will help but people procrastinate for other reasons. Do the drudgery work first.

Train Yourself to Listen
We have all worked with difficult people. Just listen without any editorial comments. They will feel better and you will have reduced the stress-time.

Increase Collaboration
Lichen is a plant found in high elevation northern climates. It is made up of algae and fungus, two separate biological entities that combined to survive in a stressful environment. Fungus supplies support and water for the algae and algae furnishes food to the fungus. This system works for us too.

Change-Up on Tasks
The body can take only so much stress on one part before complaining, so change the task for awhile. Shifting the stress helps relax the other body system.

Think About Work Differently
George Bernard Shaw said that work is doing what we must and leisure is doing what we like. We agree, but if we tell ourself that we like work, it reduces the stress.

Twenty-minute Down Time
This is done at home. Tell your family that you need 20 minutes of rest when you get home before starting the next round of duties. Do not allow any interruptions.

Stress management at work is no different from personal techniques used in other settings. You will notice that these 15 ideas give you all kinds of general statements with respect to relieving your stress. We want to be emphatic about the fact that relationship and communication skills at work are absolutely essential, just as they are necessary in all other settings. Somehow we tend to be less personable at work because we are either very busy or we separate work from other aspects of our life. Nevertheless, the ideas that we present have been known to work. For example, we know that if you increase the rate at which you praised other colleagues at work you would certainly get more of that positive feedback yourself. Self-organization, time management and avoiding the politics and procrastination are all good ideas but we have to decide that these are the things that we want to do and try. Our personality and temperament often get in the way of taking that first step towards change. Be that as it may, we cannot be too rigid or we will always be feeling stress. Train yourself to listen, use the two minute relaxer, change tasks within the limits of your work setting and try, as much as you can, to use the twenty minute down-time at the end of the day. We have found that this particular strategy is one of the most helpful. After a twenty minute down-time we can listen to the children's concerns or go about our home duties, such as meal time preparation or cutting the lawn, and feel energized doing them. Study the list once more and then write out five strategies that you can try on your own. On the following blank page you will be able to select your five strategies, write them down and indicate specific ways in which you can make it work in your particular setting.

My   Success   with   Stress   Worksheet

Reduce Aggressiveness and Increase Assertiveness

There are pushy people around and most of us do not like them. These are people who pester and nag, push and shove, fight and aggress and are generally rude and obnoxious individuals. Aggressive people have the need to be in control. They get what they want by being pushy but at what a terrific cost! Now we must keep in mind that there are times when we should all be aggressive. I think it is necessary to be aggressive about: pursuing freedom from abuse, desiring a spirit of peace, seeking freedom from bad habits, letting go of young adult children, striving for justice, fighting for happiness and pushing away loneliness. Pushing or pulling, getting help wherever possible and getting what you want, provided you are not hurting each other in the process, is not aggression. We encourage aggression if the values are there for justice, love, peace and happiness for self and others. We discourage aggression if you hurt others while pushing for what you want.

People use many different ways of getting what they want. Some use reason and logic. They tend to give you multiple reasons for their particular point of view. Others use friendliness. They make you feel worthy and wanted. They get what they want through their politeness. Still others use coalition. They obtain support of other people towards their own goals. Still others appeal to higher authority. They have no problems in going to a superior and getting support for a certain matter. Others bargain. These people propose deals and compromise so that they can get their way. We all use these strategies from time to time. However, research has shown that our upbringing as well as our personality and experiences cause us to use certain approaches more often than others. In the main, we find that neither the shotgun approach nor the tactical approach, neither the ingratiators nor the combiners, work effectively all the time.

People who are aggressive are seen very negatively by others. Both men and women are viewed equally negatively. While men tend to use reason and logic more often than women, women tend to be the persuaders. Women who use logic and reasoning to get what they want are not viewed highly in the workplace. This has been supported by a number of research studies. In fact, it is true to say that women who use friendliness and ingratiation are valued the most because people tend to like women who use such an approach. We still have a double standard in our world today. It seems that men's ideas are valued over women's ideas. Clearly, this is a sexist view. What we are suggesting is that we should learn to be assertive rather than aggressive except in the cases of aggression noted above.

Learning to be assertive allows us to effectively say no when we need to, and it allows us to be firm yet gentle. So how can we learn to be more assertive? Here are some differences between the assertive person and the aggressive person. This chart will help you place yourself in one category or the other.

Assertiveness	*Aggressiveness*
Gives straight forward, honest answers	Gives aggressive answers
Is firm, not loud	Is aggressive in decision-making
Holds ground resolutely	Is loud and super-firm
Admits mistakes	Holds ground angrily
Has a definite plan and goal and follows them without stepping on others	Denies faults
Knows what is wanted and lets others know	Has goals but steps on others to achieve them
Is patient and goal oriented	Is often aggressive with a plan
Is self-confident most of the time	Is impatient while still goal-oriented
Has high self-esteem	Is often unsure, hence the aggression
	Often has low self-esteem

Can you see the difference between people who are assertive and people who are aggressive? Assertiveness is a skill and it can be learned. People who are assertive tend to use reason, are friendly and make bargains. While they still can be authoritative on some issues they tend to seek coalition and are more tactful. They use the language of diplomacy. On the other hand, people who are aggressive tend to yell and want their own way, and are basically unfriendly toward others without the authority to be so.

Learning to be more assertive may require an entire weekend workshop somewhere, but we think that there is a way in which you can begin right now. Try the following strategies:

Assertive Strategies

1. Examine yourself to see whether or not you are more assertive than aggressive. If you are already leaning on the assertive side then continue with that skill.

2. Begin believing in yourself. Say out loud to yourself, "I believe in myself," but also let others know that you believe in who you are and what you stand for.

3. Develop clear and reasonable goals for your work setting. Know what you want to do and how much you want to do each day, and make these goals reasonable.

4. Take small steps in achieving your goals. Don't try to short circuit the process.

5. Compromise when it is needed. There are times when you feel that you are right but by compromising you will get further in the long run.

6. Be open and honest and use direct talk. Speak from the hip and the lip.

7. Think and plan ahead. Know where you are heading and be prepared for your work as well as for meetings in your work setting.

8. Seek advice. It helps to appear to be humble even if you are not. Give in when the advice seems solid and reasonable.

People who are persistently aggressive have the need for control and influence. Their stress levels are much higher than assertive types. Using a less vigorous influence style is more healthy and reduces the level of stress. There are times, however, when you have no choice and need to be aggressive. But those times should be few and far between. Assertive people often use a "let me think about it" style. They honestly do think about it, gather more information and then come back with an answer. While sudden decisions are necessary at times, in most cases you can delay them until you have thought about it. Many times a reflective answer is better than the first impulsive one. Decide ahead of time on the issues in which you simply will not give in and then follow your strategy. Most of us do not need assertiveness training. The few simple ideas presented here should help you towards that path and will assist in reducing stress in the workplace.

When Solutions to Problems are Hard to Find

All of us would agree that hardly a day goes by that we do not have at least one or two problems to solve, whether with our children, spouse, work, colleagues, or finances. One way to look at it is that these things are quite normal. Dr. M. Scott Peck, in his book **The Road Less Travelled**, urges his readers to take the attitude that problems are part of daily living. If we hold this attitude then it makes it easier to accept the situation. Say to yourself, "So here's another day. I wonder what problems I have to solve today? Let's see, today my problems are thus and thus. Let's work on some of the solutions." With this attitude you will not be so susceptible to letting the daily problems pile up, or affect you emotionally. Too often, we take the attitude, "Oh no - another problem...Can't anything ever go right? I don't want to ever have this problem again!" But there are times and there are problems for which solutions are hard to find because of their complexity or because the person is in no condition to look for a solution. Sometimes the solutions are hard to find because the resources are simply not there. Here are three possible techniques that could be used for just these situations:

Technique No. 1
Stress Appraisal: Two Column Technique

Anxiety Thoughts	Alternative Interpretation
I have a fear of being fired.	No supervisor has even hinted that I may be let go.
I have a feeling that someone is being aloof and avoiding me.	Person X is aloof to everyone, not just to me.
Staff stop their conversation in the coffee room whenever I walk in.	There is a real status difference here. Fortunately I have a few good friends on staff.

Now write down some of your anxiety thoughts and alternative interpretations.

My Anxiety Thoughts	My Alternative Interpretation
1)	1)
2)	2)
3)	3)
4)	4)
5)	5)
6)	6)
7)	7)
8)	8)
9)	9)
10)	10)
11)	11)
12)	12)
13)	13)

Technique No. 2
Stress Appraisal: Three Column Technique

OBJECTIVE DATA	MY AUTOMATIC THOUGHTS	POSSIBLE ERRORS
Describe the stress-producing situations	Write down your automatic thought	Analyze your thoughts for possible errors
For example: *All the fun has gone out* *of my job.* *I do not enjoy going* *to work.*	*Is it mid-life crisis?* *I'm bored with my routines.* *There's no chance of* *promotion.*	*I'm too young for a crisis.* *I have some choices.* *I should ask about promotion.*

Now fill in your objective data, your automatic thoughts about the data and the possible errors in your thoughts.

Objective Data

_____

_____

_____

My Automatic Thoughts

_____

_____

_____

Possible Errors

_____

_____

_____

Technique No. 3
The A - W - A - R - E Technique

Understanding your perception of and reaction to an event is as helpful as most stress-coping techniques. The following steps, represented by the acronym AWARE, can be quickly memorized and used on every stress-producing situation or thought:

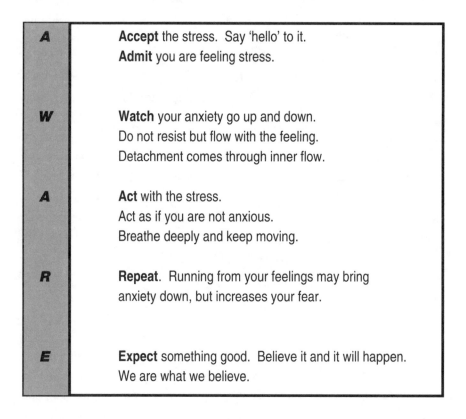

A	**Accept** the stress. Say 'hello' to it. **Admit** you are feeling stress.
W	**Watch** your anxiety go up and down. Do not resist but flow with the feeling. Detachment comes through inner flow.
A	**Act** with the stress. Act as if you are not anxious. Breathe deeply and keep moving.
R	**Repeat**. Running from your feelings may bring anxiety down, but increases your fear.
E	**Expect** something good. Believe it and it will happen. We are what we believe.

On the preceding three pages were three individual problem-solving techniques. These do take time to work through but are effective in reducing stress by finding another way to look at the problem. Everyone can learn to take an active role in doing something productive that leads to coping effectively with stress in the workplace.

The techniques you have just read ask you to look at the questions, "What's the evidence? What does this situation look like? What does it demand of me?" In other words, you are asked to ask yourself, "How do I look at this?" Secondly, you are asked to find another way of looking at the problem. By looking for alternate interpretations you are saying to yourself, "Am I jumping to conclusions? Am I right or wrong? Are my emotions in line with the situation? Is there another way of looking at it?" And thirdly, you are asked to look at the questions, "So what if it happens? What is my prediction of the outcome? Am I basing my prediction on past evidence or a feeling? Am I utilizing all the information available?" This is a way of analyzing specific problems and the emotions and causes behind them.

By taking the time to go through these techniques you will find new answers that may relieve your stress. Not all of life's difficult challenges can be planned for, but if we have an attitude of openness it makes these challenges easier to bear. Nothing hinders the road to recovery more than an unwillingness to be open and honest with ourselves. Without this openness and honesty, the solutions may be entirely wrong, dealing with incorrect aspects of the problem. Flexibility, some psychologists say, is a natural trait. Some people are more flexible than others. We can learn to alter our ways. We do not have to give up our values or morals to be flexible. We just need to be willing to examine ourselves, to look for alternatives and possibly to compromise.

How many times have we heard people say, "I've tried this and that and nothing seems to help!" Why this road block? Why are the solutions so hard to find? Partly it is because we are dealing with so many variables and complexities of any one problem, and partly it is because of change in our world. Research has found that as we make one small change, changes occur all along the way; changes occur in the entire system. So we must start somewhere. We are asking each of you to start with yourself and to look at some of your ways of thinking and reasoning. As you attempt the Two-Column and the Three-Column techniques you will find that you do have the resources within to find solutions and to make those changes that are deemed necessary for effectively reducing stress.

And finally, technique number three, the **A-W-A-R-E technique**, will help you understand your problems and reactions. The **A-W-A-R-E technique** is useful in controlling an intense emotional reaction to a situation at work or home. Memorize those five letters of the alphabet in the word A-W-A-R-E and what they stand for. You will find it a freeing technique.

Managers and Executives Who cope Well

Much of the stress in business management is produced by difficult relationships between people at work and by the inner responses to these situations. People in management must take responsibility for the way individuals react to authority and power. Without a doubt, certain styles of management also can cause stress, some in very predictable ways. Of course, there may be no perfect solutions to all this, but as managers we should try to be very sensitive to signs of stress such as: absenteeism, altered moods, self-isolation, increased alcoholism, mid-career burnout and increased tensions and conflicts. People in management have to be quite sensitive to personality differences. Research has shown that individual personality types react very differently to stress. So we have to begin a process to help executives understand employees people and each other better.

One other thing needs to be mentioned in this preamble. There are studies that have shown that it is pure myth that people in management are under a tremendous amount of pressure. Harry Truman's favourite description of the presidency of the United States was "The buck stops here." The tradition of command may be a lonely occupation where "love flees authority." We have found in our own work in business and industry that managers are no more vulnerable to stress than anyone else. In fact, managers who had high responsibility but low authority were the ones that were under far more stress than the top executives. These are the middle-managers, the ones with low order management responsibilities. Individuals in roles of authority are no better able to cope with stress than anyone else either. However, people in authority do have the bureaucratic ability to produce stress. Therefore, one must recognize at the outset that anything that can be done to involve people in making decisions and increase their personal self-esteem, while not necessarily removing the stress, will give increased power to those individuals to cope with their stress more effectively. In the next table some ideas on coping with the situation by increasing employee self-control are outlined.

Increasing Employee Self-Control

Try these!

1. Find every opportunity for employees to work independently.
2. Offer employees opportunity for greater responsibility.
3. Let employees decide what really is required of them. Let them build personal mission statements.
4. Offer strict control in business in areas of service and efficiency. The rest will take care of themselves.
5. Build greater harmony by employee participation in decision-making and organization mission statement development.
6. Allow employees to manage their own personal leave time (sick, vacation, personal business, holidays).
7. Allow employees (or encourage) personal initiatives relative to the business.
8. Allow a two-hour flexible start and leave work arrangement. As long as the hours are covered, the employees will work shifts to suit them and profit the business.
9. Provide an opportunity for someone to develop or contribute to a company newsletter, giving recognition to those doing a good job.
10. Every year offer the opportunity for employees to learn a new task or skill.
11. Let employees know of the exact financial situation of the business. When times are good it develops pride. When times are bad it encourages faithfulness.
12. Above all, develop a friendly and happy atmosphere in the workplace.
13. Offer Employee Assistance Programs as a number one priority. Everybody has problems and stress and that will affect the business.
14. Job security is not always possible, but do give the nod to faithful employees - regardless of productivity.
15. Everybody needs to feel a sense of personal accomplishment, so give opportunity in some way for employees to "brag" about themselves.

Increasing employee self-control is a matter of individual choice but every one of these things can assist managers in making their employees feel a personal sense of mission within the business. Managers and executives who have increased employee participation in decision-making, who have allowed employees to manage their own personal leave time, or who have been more flexible with respect to start and leave work arrangements, have relatively fewer major issues to solve in their business. We have seen these strategies work within small and large companies in this country. Study each of the above suggestions carefully and decide which ones you would feel comfortable implementing.

Success-Thinking in the Workplace

Every manager or executive will find one or two behaviour patterns in an employee that make that employee difficult to manage. Many of you will be familiar with hostile and aggressive people who try to bully and overwhelm others by making cutting remarks or throwing temper tantrums. Some of you will have complainers in your business who gripe incessantly but never do anything about their complaints. Others will find the silent and unresponsive employees who question everything you do. There are even the super-agreeables who are funny and outgoing and who sound very reasonable and sincere, but act contrary to the way you would expect. And then who has not met the know-it-all experts? These are those 'superior' people who want you to recognize that they know everything there is to know about anything worth knowing. And then there are the indecisive ones who stall major decisions until the decision is made for them. They are also the same ones who cannot let go of anything until it is perfect. Executives who cope well with these various situations have used some of the following strategies.

Management Strategies

1. The Magic Circle.

When holding staff meetings, use a magic circle. Have employees sit in circular fashion rather than at square or rectangular tables. In the magic circle technique all individuals are allowed to express their ideas free of negation or caustic remarks. Criticism of any comment is not allowed. This ventilation of feelings works to let the steam out. If you find that you hit a road block, simply move on and get away from that problem or idea for a while and then come back to it later. Do not stand your ground all the time, even in situations where you are certain that the other person is wrong. Yielding, according to stress research, reduces a lot of strain on your nervous system and pays off in better relationships in the future. And finally, avoid perfection. Too many capable individuals tie themselves in knots and are less effective because they are seeking perfection. Stress is reduced if the orientation is towards what was accomplished rather than what was not. It is the process that you go through that is really more important than the solution itself. When people see that the process is fair, their emotional reactions to it decrease and the stress is reduced.

2. Planning Factors

Since much of our stress in management is produced within ourselves, planning a process as mentioned above is clearly the answer. Planning will include clear visualization of present and future goals. There must be a time when every company has to involve employees in developing their own personal mission statements and the mission statements of the organization. This process will take an evening or a day from work but it is indeed a very careful and structured activity that gives individuals a sense of pride in what they do. The authors have used this process of writing personal as well as organizational mission statements with companies who found a positive outcome every time. Once individuals understand their own personal values and priorities in life, and those of the organization, they can blend them together. The individuals then become attached to the place where they work and work much harder. This reduces the stress in the organization.

3. Go With the Flow

Executives who cope well invent ways to challenge themselves. They see their work much like a hobby and they also know how to match their skill to the job. Going with the flow, therefore, refers to knowing your strengths and having realistic expectations. Instead of trying to charge forward on a path that you think is proper for yourself, find ways to show the enjoyment of what you do, and ask others their opinions. Going with the flow is being sensitive to the response of those individuals who work for you.

4. Optimistic Management Style

Executives who cope well with stress see the glass half-full and not half-empty. Every executive may have had tough days but these ones always say to themselves that things will get better. This is a way of stopping those negative thoughts, realizing mistakes have but a temporary effect and refusing to blame ourself for failures. Positive thinking does not allow mistakes and mishaps to infringe upon other areas of life. Visualizing what you did well in the past and then having a vision for the future, combined with interacting with others, will give you this optimism. When a bad thought comes into your mind, simply shout "STOP" and then insert a positive thought.

5. Flexible Thinking

Creative lateral thinking, such as those found in a De Bono technique, has been known to people in business for a long time. We recall when the Firestone Company wanted to develop new tires they utilized this technique. They got all their people together and each person was randomly given five different words out of the dictionary. The executive then went forward and wrote the specific problem on the blackboard, namely, to develop a new tire. Everyone was to look at the five words that had been randomly selected and try to apply these words to the problem in whatever way they could. This strategy forced lateral thinking and produced much creativity in solving problems. The process also brought excitement to the company and to the individual.

6. Managing Time and Work Your Way

Executives who cope well find that they have very different strategies in the way they handle their work but they are able to do it quite effectively. Some executives are more right-brained people. They relish talking ideas over, keeping all the papers in sight, and taking joy breaks. They are the people who can drink, relax and think of bringing flowers home to their wives. On the other hand, we have those executives who are more left-brained thinkers. These people like to make lists, handle details and put things back in neat piles where they found them. Left-brained people like to handle paper only once and finish A before starting B. Managing time 'your way' is finding out which strategy works best for you. The best way to use time on certain occasions is to ignore the clock. For example, in an automobile industry one executive said that while it takes seventeen minutes to replace the brakes on a 1983 Dodge, it is more important to take even more time to deal with a client. This produces far more service and business in the future. Managing time 'your way' is working on this brain balance. By doing this you bring personal enthusiasm, fun and energy into your business.

7. Managing the Environment

The work environment is as important as the work itself. Employees must like the environment where they work. Just as they arrange their home to suit their personal needs, allow them to arrange the work environment in certain ways to make it more comfortable for them. Clearly, lighting and noise factors are important. These things have to be taken care of immediately. Give your employees freedom to make decisions on arranging the environment. If you have certain ideas yourself, offer them--but with diplomacy. If somebody, for example, would like to have an office near a window, then try to accommodate that request. Another way to arrange the environment is to make somebody in charge of editing a newsletter. Personal information can be gleaned from others. Personal accomplishments should be reinforced in the newsletter and outside evening and weekend activities could be listed. Socializing on the job is as important for a happy business as anything else. These are all external factors relative to the environment but they improve the internal attitude.

Managers and executives who cope well with stress are people with a vision of personal leadership. Leadership is not just management. Leadership is the first priority. Perhaps you can see it in another way. Management asks the question, "How can I best accomplish things?" But leadership asks the question, "What are the things I want to accomplish?" Peter Drucker once said that management is doing things right while leadership is doing the right things. There is a very important difference here. We need managers who have leadership qualities that involve vision. This vision requires a compass and a set of principles that will always give direction. If leaders do not have this vision they will be like people straightening out the deck chairs on the Titanic while it is sinking.

The leader is the one who should climb the tallest tree and survey the entire situation. Unfortunately, sometimes the leader discovers that they are all in the wrong jungle. If that is so, then very important changes will have to be made. Executives and managers who cope well with stress are able to build their own self-esteem and the self-esteem of those for whom they are responsible in the workplace. They are people who live by the principle of guidance; that is, they have an inner map and a source of direction in life, but they share it with others and allow others to contribute to it. We have already suggested that you take the time to write personal mission statements with your employees.

Managers who cope well with stress also have wisdom. Wisdom is that balance between knowledge and experience. Both are needed to survive in the business world today.

Henry Ward Beecher, a famous preacher of the 18th century, was once buying a horse. He saw a fine animal and asked the owner about it. The owner told him that it was a great horse who would work any place, go when you wanted to, stop when you said and be perfectly gentle yet full of spirit. The horse had no bad traits, would not bite or kick and would come when you called. It would never run off. Reverend Beecher then said, "If only that horse were a member in my business."

We all want people like that in our business so it is time to stop and think about who we are and how we do things. This involves taking stock of ourselves, our organization and the people with whom we are involved with. While our work and our business gives us our livelihood, we must always place that in perspective. In Chapter Two we said that we need to think about taking stock in terms of a balance in our life: a balance between our work, our family, our social life and our leisure time. It is not healthy to focus our world on only one centre or even two centres. We must strike a balance between all of them. This will involve a new way of thinking about our work as well. Work is an important centre of our life but it cannot be the most important. Money is an important centre of our life but it cannot be the most important either. Even our family, church, spouse and possessions are very important centres of our life but they too cannot be the sole focus. We must have a balance. What we are suggesting is that if you choose to live your life by the principles of wisdom and guidance as well as self-esteem building, you will reduce the stressors in yourself and in the workplace.

Chapter Five

BALANCING HOME AND WORK

Working couples have become a fact of life today. Over 58.4% of women are now in the work force. In the case of co-habiting couples, over 90% of people in those relationships work outside of the home. Today we have less than 25% of the traditional nuclear family left in Canada. What we have indicated up to this point is that there are a number of stress management techniques that can be used. The short-term techniques are those that are used to regulate your emotions during stress while the long-term strategies are those that you need to implement for the bigger problems or stressors. While we do not need to repeat those suggestions in this chapter, we want to let you know that from time to time there may be some overlap.

Balancing home and work is a problem for all couples that are working outside of the home. In a sense, the long-term strategy suggested in Chapter Five, namely that of taking stock and balancing the four quadrants of life, is what we are going to suggest you do here. Before we do that, however, let us discuss some of the advantages and disadvantages to the husband, wife and children when both spouses are working outside of the home.

Advantages to the Husband

Let it be clear that we are talking about side advantages to the husband when the wife works outside of the home rather than advantages to the husband for working outside of the home himself. A husband whose spouse works outside of the home gains freedom because a working spouse gives the couple greater financial resources. This situation also allows either spouse to change or leave their job and risk going into some new venture. When more money comes into the home there is often reduced emotional tension. Also, there is more to talk about. When a spouse works outside of the home she is exposed to other people's ideas. This sharing of ideas broadens the range of issues for conversation. In the past, when the wife worked only in the home, the husband could come home to an earful of routine issues regarding the children, job jar complaints, financial pressures or social outings. Now the wife understands the stressors that the husband faces at work. Often this makes their relationship more compatible.

Another significant advantage to the husband having a spouse working outside of the home is his increased role in parenting. While not all husbands take on this challenge, today more do than ever before. Men have now learned to enjoy their children by spending more quality time with them. One man in my private practice told me, "I can relax a little, spend more time with the children and keep up with inflation." While it may be inconvenient for some families to have both spouses working outside of the home, it can bring greater happiness in life style and relationship.

Advantages to the Wife

Again, we are talking about the advantages accruing to the spouse herself when she works outside of the home rather than the advantages accruing to the husband.

The things that we are about to suggest are ideas taken from research. Galambos and Walters (1992) compared the responses of working outside of the home wives, working in the home wives and the unmarried but working women. From these responses, the researchers suggest that the main advantage accruing to a spouse in working outside of the home is increased self-esteem and personal confidence. Women who work outside of the home reported feeling more attractive, less lonely and even being more effective in child-rearing than when they were working in the home. You see, these women felt that working outside of the home gave them recognition for their talents and gifts. It utilized their energy, education, experience and abilities. Indeed, the spouse felt that she could support herself, but what she was really saying was that she felt far more independent.

While co-dependency in a relationship is certainly valuable and present in most circumstances, too much dependency on each other will eventually breed mild if not major hostilities. Furthermore, the 'empty nest syndrome' had less effect on the women working outside of the home. Most couples can cope with their children leaving home but those that work outside of the home find this an easier adjustment to make. This information is reinforced by John Freedman in his book **Happy People**. Freedman said that "women who work outside of the home feel much happier. They fuss less about muddy boots and husbands being late for dinner."

Advantages to the Children

It might seem quite contradictory to suggest that there are advantages to the children when both parents work outside of the home. Nevertheless, there are advantages.

Indirectly, by more money coming into the home, children are able to get that extra pair of boots, the hockey equipment, those skis and whatever else money can buy. Children themselves report that there is less tension in the home when both parents work because money is still the number one reason for fighting. The home appears to be based on a more equal relationship with both parents working. The children do not feel smothered by 'Super Mom,' nor pampered by Dad who never does the disciplining. Both parents share more equitably when helping their children with their homework. In the past, children felt much like Annie who hung around with her mother at the theatre all the time. At one point Annie said of all these people in the theatre, "Don't they have anything else to do?" Annie recognized that adults enjoy their work and that is why they spend so much time at it. Children learn to accept new career ideas as they grow up and take greater pride in their parents' jobs.

The Balancing Act

Here are a few ideas that are helpful in combating the stressors when both parents work outside of the home. We recognize the fatigue and understand the different levels of energy that may create tensions when one person wants to rest and the other wants to go out. We empathize with those people who feel that a big problem in their sex life exsists when their spouse goes to bed at a different time than they do. What we are about to suggest are things that are essential in keeping the relationship between the spouses alive and the home life healthy and happy.

Talking, Discussing and Communicating

When both parents work outside of the home the best thing they can do when they both come home is to sit down and have some *down time*. This means that both spouses take 20 minutes to sit down with a soft drink, tea or coffee and debrief each other on the day's events. It is important for the spouses not to be involved with mind reading or trying to figure out just what the other person needs and feels. Open and honest discussion of feelings including pressures, successes and failures will improve the relationship and help each of you feel better. While debriefing, it is probably more important not to ask questions but to simply state wants or feelings such as, "I feel like going to a movie tonight" or "I had a bad day at work today."

You see, questions create hidden agendas while statements of wants and feelings do not. The other person knows exactly where you are coming from. Stating feelings also suggests that you do not state facts. It is better to say, "I'm cold" rather than "It's too cold in here." It is better to say, "I don't like the way the house looks" rather than "This house is a mess." It is better to say, "I don't like yellow" instead of "Yellow is an ugly colour." By stating feelings you find a more receptive ear. Thinking about what you want to say, taking the time to debrief at the end of the day and then discussing it is very important. Communication implies that you have understood what the other person has said. By stating your feelings openly and honestly there can be less chance of mind reading and misleading perceptions.

Balancing the Power

Men have had their share of power in relationships for longer than women care to mention. However, most marriages work best if that power is equalized in one way or another. Those of you raised in the Christian tradition believe that the man is the head of the household. It is said that the man must love his wife and the woman must love the husband and be subject to him. While it is true that both the Old and New Testaments directed women to submit to their husbands, this was never meant to be interpreted as slavery. The word subjection does not mean "to obey," but "to arrange in order." This means that the balance of power, while it may reside in different roles and obligations, is an equal share of responsibility in which the woman, even in the Christian tradition, is to see subjection as simply "arranging in order to do those things that must be done to take care of the household."

It is certainly true that women have greater stress when they work outside of the home because many of them have greater responsibilities than the man in the home. This finding was made very clear by Dr. Gerry Long who investigated the role of women in the work force in his doctoral dissertation. While balancing the power may be tough to do, it is something that has to be carefully planned in advance and discussed without intense emotions before it can happen. The woman can certainly ask the question, "Whose dirty floors are they anyway?" Love does not clean the floors. Love cleans up one's own mess. So balancing the power means negotiating roles and goals in a systematic way. Find time to sit down when you are calm and relaxed and discuss who does what. You will agree that this is far better than the work not getting done or one person internalizing frustrations for weeks and then exploding later. Sit down and discuss the jobs that have to be done. Involve the children as well. You may want to give someone the task of personal maintenance which would include arranging the dentist appointments for the children, taking care of the bills, having the cars fixed or doing the grocery shopping.

It is also sensible to reduce the number of chores that have to be done. A little bit of compromise will have to happen here, especially if one spouse is a bit compulsive about neatness. If there are some jobs that are worse than others, then simply decide to take turns doing them. Hire a cleaning lady if you can afford it. Set priorities. Give up the "Better Homes and Gardens" ideal. And finally, look for shortcuts simply for efficiency. Some shortcuts include the idea that all household members can take care of their own personal laundry and hygiene. Purchase comforters that can be thrown on the bed instead of worrying about who will make the bed. Buy groceries in bulk to eliminate frequent shopping trips. Purchase long cords for the phone or use a cordless phone so that you can walk around the house while doing some chores. This increases efficiency.

Balancing the power means avoiding exploitation and guilt. No marriage can stand an unbalanced relationship. We cannot have one horse and one rabbit and suggest that this is an equal balance of power.

Working Parents and the Effect on Children

There are both positive and negative aspects of working outside of the home. While we do not want to focus on the negatives as much, we do want you to know that there are some that have to be considered. For example, grandparents may be very judgemental about both parents working outside of the home because this simply was not done in their day. Parents may feel guilt, especially the wife. Another negative aspect may be that the children are more indulged financially with less time taken for discipline and outings. When both parents work outside of the home children are often less helpful because parents are not around to see that the chores and studies get done. This creates another problem of what should be done when children do not do the jobs that they were assigned.

But there are far more positive effects when both parents work. The fact is, research shows that most children turn out just fine with both parents working outside of the home. Great men of the past like Winston Churchill, George Bernard Shaw and Bertrand Russell had both parents working outside the home. Working parents recognize that children still need their time and care but the time that they now spend with them is more effective and efficient. You may want to call it quality time. The well-known expert in child psychology, Dr. Jerome Kagan at Harvard University, said that children need to feel valued and have stability and predictability. The fact is that the best care parents can give to their children is to love each other first, and then love their children. This can happen when both parents work outside of the home.

Children do need time with both parents but when both are working, children tend to equalize their attention rather than focusing it all on the spouse who is working in the home. When parents work outside of the home they tend to communicate and interact more with their children than ever before, probably because they feel a bit guilty. When parents work outside of the home they structure their time with their children so it becomes a more effective and efficient way of interacting. For example, there is nothing wrong with taking your children to your workplace, if it can be arranged. We have done this for years and it has been one of the most pleasant by-products for our children. Our children have learned so much of what we do through this practice. Children still need supervision, and there is daycare as well as other programs that can adequately take care of our children. What we want to avoid are the situations where children come home to an empty house at a very young age and have no one to call on in times of need. Latch-key children do have a difficult time adjusting.

Finally, there have to be special arrangements made by one or the other spouse when school is out early, when the children need medical attention or when the children are home sick. As you can see, the effect on children need not be negative.

Balanced Care of the Relationship

Up to this point we have mentioned some key strategies that will help you balance home and work. We now want to focus on the relationship between the spouses when they are both working. Many times the writer has heard people say that one spouse is far more tired than the other and therefore goes to bed early, or one spouse has to get up very early in the morning and thus goes to bed well before the other. This situation alone will cause some tension and eventually some problems in the marriage unless it is accommodated.

Balanced care takes a lot of hard work. The basics of any solid relationship are in the respect for each other, tolerance for differences, flexibility in allowing for uniqueness, commitment to each other for life and the sharing of power. To have balanced care in the relationship means that both partners have to be open to each other's needs and feelings. There are times when one may have to compromise more than the other, but basically each spouse has a responsibility for daily re-entry into the home. Daily re-entry may take the form of a debriefing session each day or, as we have called it, 'down time.' Another aspect of balancing the care of the relationship is that roles and goals in the family have to be re-negotiated a few times a year so that everyone can take responsibility for doing some of the hard jobs.

Everyone in the family will experience stress but not everyone copes with it the same way. To take care of the stressors of work and home as well as individual family members, it helps to sense these pressures early. When we come home with a headache, low back pain, excessive fatigue and nervousness, it makes sense that we recognize these pressures and tell others about them so that the family can step in and help out a little more than they otherwise might have.

It also makes sense to learn and practice stress coping techniques. Turn to chapter two and try some of the short-term ideas for reducing your emotional level and the long-term ideas for coping with some of the major problems. Balanced care in the relationship when both spouses are working outside of the home allows each spouse some relaxation time when he or she needs it. It might involve lowering your expectations about what the other spouse can do. It will certainly mean that no major changes are going to be made when the stress is heavy.

Balancing The Four Major Life-Quadrants

Balancing home and work will require this little exercise. You might want to turn to the next two pages just to see what we are talking about. We have set out four major quadrants that need to be balanced if you want to experience less stress.

Here is all you have to do:

1. Take some time to estimate the percentage of time that each of you are currently spending on each quadrant.
2. List those activities in each quadrant that you currently do and check your responses against those of your spouse.
3. Compare notes and revise.

We feel that on a second page it is important for you to revise your previous estimates after you and your spouse have discussed them. It is normal for couples to spend at least 60% of their time outside of the home and then divide the time in the remaining three quadrants as they see fit. Clearly you have to give some time for leisure and social activities and each family may have different percentages here. There is no magic in the balancing act. It is more important, however, for you to take the time to do this simply because we are often unaware of how much time we give to each of these quadrants. It will make sense to you when you realize that you may be spending very little time in recreation, exercise and relaxation. We need that quadrant to maintain a healthy life style and reduce the stress. We feel that home and work by and large consume the majority of people's time. Work is the place where we get our financial resources and therefore it becomes a priority, but what about the idea that the home should receive greater priority? Most families would agree to this. In fact, today many more working spouses give the home far greater priority because they now see how important it is in relation to their work. So take the time right now to go through the four major life-quadrants and follow the instructions at the bottom of the page.

Balancing The Four Major Life-Quadrants

HOME	WORK
Family, children, extended family, etc.	Business, job, travel, studies, etc.
LEISURE	**SOCIAL**
Recreation, exercise, relaxing, reading, television, etc.	Friends over, church activities, service clubs, dinners out, movies, etc. - all with friends

1. Study the quadrants and estimate the percentage of time you spend in each.
2. List those activities in each quadrant you currently do.
3. Check your responses against those of your spouse.
4. Compare notes and revise.

Your Four Major Life-Quadrants

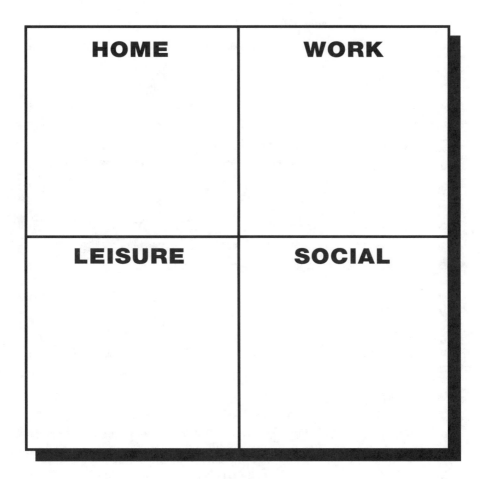

1. Use this page to revise your previous estimates. Remember that in a normal 7:00 a.m. to 11:00 p.m. day, it is the norm to have up to 60% of your time devoted to work. Of the remaining three quadrants, try to find up to 20 % for HOME and 10% each for LEISURE and SOCIAL activities.

Women's Changing Work Roles

Women, and their families, are undergoing a natural experiment of enormous proportions. Early in Canada's history, women worked long, hard hours primarily within their own homes or farms. By the turn of this century, around 20% were working outside the home. These women were usually single or widowed. Very few had careers. During World War II, many women had to be recruited into the work force. Although some women left the work force after the war, many remained and their numbers have continued to increase ever since. These demographic shifts and major changes in women's roles at work impacted on their home, their relationships in and outside of the home and their mental and physical health.

One of the things that many women experience when they decide to work outside of the home is guilt. Guilt can come even if the husband has indicated that he is quite supportive about the spouse working outside the home. But let us look at this problem of guilt and find some ways to solve it.

What is Guilt?

Guilt is an emotion as well as a thought that comes from doing something that we think is wrong or bad. Guilt can also come when we feel we are not doing something that we feel ought to be done. This absence of an appropriate response can also make us feel guilty. Guilt is never an instinctive reaction. Children need to be capable of moral reasoning, usually around the age of six, before they can experience guilt. At the core of guilt is a feeling that we have let ourselves and others down. In other words, guilt usually refers to the personal experience you have when you feel your internal standards have been broken. Thus, guilt can take the expression of feeling to blame for something we have not done right.

Guilt is also associated with perceptions of ability. By this we mean that guilt can come when we think we can do certain things but have never been able to do them, and now that we do them we feel guilty. And then there is the spiritual guilt which comes from feeling that we have let God down in some way or another. At the core of guilt is always a loss of self-esteem, and the resultant emotions induce shame, fear, anxiety, worry and stress. It can become so consuming that you cannot sleep at night. So, what can we do?

Resolving the Problem of Guilt

CONFESSION

How many times have you heard it said that "Confession is good for the soul"? Many times, in the privacy of our professional practice, we have heard people say, "I've never told anybody about this,but I've got to get it off my chest." Just the act of talking about it does help relieve the guilt. Sharing our concerns with others is a good idea. It helps if you first share it with your spouse but often a close friend, a pastor or priest will do. While just talking about it may not solve the problem, it will lessen the pressure inside and release those stored-up feelings.

FORGIVENESS

Some people feel guilty when they work outside the home, even though nothing needs to be forgiven here, especially if both spouses have discussed it and agreed upon it. However, forgiveness is a component of guilt reduction. We should practice it regularly in our daily routine. Forgiveness involves not just forgiving the person who may have done some wrong, but forgiving yourself for imperfections. The act of forgiveness is better accomplished if it is stated verbally to another person. The other person, therefore, must accept the statement that has been made, be willing to put it in the past and forget it.

True forgiveness means that the other person will no longer count this act against you. Forgiveness must be sincere or it will not work. Just saying "I'm sorry" is often not enough. Behaving in line with expectations is needed to make forgiveness a successful treatment of guilt.

CORRECTING THE WRONG

When guilt arises out of a wrongful act, you must combine confession with forgiveness and the promise of changing your actions. If we look at the experience that has produced the guilt and learn from it, we will find it easier to change a negative emotion like guilt into a positive action. The spouse who experiences the guilt must know why that experience is there before any changes can be made. This involves open and honest discussion and communication.

EXAMINING THE ISSUES

Resolving guilt is relevant to any situation. It is often very beneficial for us to ask the question why we did what we did and what were the underlying motives for it.

In other words, we are saying that you need to carefully examine the issues, gather information and perhaps get some advice from somebody else so that you fully understand what the situation is all about. In the case of guilt over the issue of working outside of the home, freely discuss the pros and cons of this situation and the basis on which a decision was made. By examining the issues from all vantage points you will find that guilt may be a misguided emotion.

LIVING A LIFE OF INTEGRITY

Guilt will always be with us as long as we live. However, we do not need to be stressed continually because of it. In essence, the best answer for resolving guilt is to live a life of integrity, a life that is balanced and positive, a life that reaches high moral standards and has positive interactions with others.

Living a life of integrity is possible when both spouses work outside of the home as long as the children's needs are met and each spouse's needs are met within the context of the workplace and the family. We are not implying that by living a life of integrity that you have to become a 'goody two-shoes.' None of us has to be that good. When both parents work outside of the home there is often less energy to do things as thoroughly as we might wish. Although this often gives us a feeling of inadequacy, we should try to hold the view that, "There but for the Grace of God go I." We must believe that a life of integrity will reduce the inner pressures of guilt. We must try to reduce the number of times we break our own internal standards. In essence, this latter point includes all the previous ones above.

Women, more so than men, have experienced guilt because they have chosen to work outside of the home. This feeling is even more intense when the husband does not think that the woman should be taking on this responsibility. But times are changing. Now more than half of all married women work outside of the home. Remember that the workplace is not necessarily more stressful than the home for women. In fact, employment is often more beneficial and less stressful. The workplace is rewarding to women in a number of ways: it enhances a woman's sense of accomplishment and self esteem, it provides new and interesting social contacts and it adds to the woman's, and her family's, financial resources. Most employed women are mothers, and mothers have unique responsibilities that involve home and child management. We now want to turn our attention to some effective strategies for home and child management.

Home and Child Management for Working Mothers

We do not believe it is a bias or indeed sexist to focus on working mothers rather than working fathers in terms of home and child care. Certainly we recognize that more fathers today are involved with home and child care than ever before. We also believe that more fathers ought to be involved in these matters. However, since many more women are in the labour force now than ever before, this has become a primary concern. Our own research has shown that women still have the greater responsibility in the home. So how can they best manage their work in the home while still working outside of the home? The facts show that mothers working outside the home work 16 to 24 hours more per week than the fathers. For mothers who had children under the age of three years, the actual time worked was over 90 hours per week. This is quite an incredible statistic. But research shows, quite fortunately we might add, that most working mothers do not see this as adding to their stress. The seeming contradiction (more hours worked, yet not stressful) is partially explained by the finding that outside work is very fulfilling and almost 'good-for-the-soul.' It could be that working mothers are more healthy than mothers working solely in the home. Yet stress of everyday living coupled with stress on the job is there. What can they do?

Take a look at the following strategies. They may be helpful.

Coping Strategies for Working Mothers

1. Re-negotiate roles.
Most of the stress appears to come from homes where working mothers have little or no spousal support. The first strategy is to carefully renegotiate the roles each spouse is to take, now that Mom is working. Decide on a plan to share the home care responsibilities: who cooks the meals on alternate days, who helps with the cleaning, who goes to school functions, etc. Negotiation is the key! Fathers are mainly upset about the inconvenience of this renegotiation of roles, but a careful routine helps bridge any problems.

2. Time management.
Time-management is essential. Have a weekly schedule planned in advance and let

each family member know of this schedule. That way, there will be no surprises or disappointments. If roles and duties are shared and everyone knows the schedule, fewer frustrations will result.

3. Find private time.

Working parents need private time. Plan for one evening out with your spouse each week. A quiet walk and talk, a candlelight dinner, an evening at the movies or any other enjoyable event calms the heart, soul, mind and body. Find a reliable babysitter. Talk about the weeks events and how you feel about each other.

4. Share your problems with your spouse.

Stressors at work need to be shared at home. Even if your spouse cannot help that much, just sharing your problems lets the feeling out. If you are a single mother meet with a friend and unburden yourself. Once a month is a good guideline for this activity.

5. Plan time for yourself.

You need at least one hour a week for a quiet time of doing exactly what your want to do: reading, going for a walk, doing your nails, having a long hot bath. This hour must be planned in advance since your week is already very full. Maybe an early Sunday morning will be needed, before anyone else gets up.

6. Attend social functions.

Stress is often reduced by social occasions. Having people over to the house just creates more work for you, so plan something else. Invite your friends to an event like a hockey game, a movie, an art show, a curling game or church event. Plan to go for coffee afterwards. Friends often help to unburden us. They provide a respite from our daily work. This should happen at least once or twice a month.

7. Feel good about yourself.

Parents need to feel good about themselves before they can help their children feel good about themselves. You can be tired but still feel good about yourself. Knowing you have planned the weeks activities, take time to be with your children. It is not how much time you take, just the quality of that time. Ten minutes a day is helpful, if children have your undivided attention. Remember, you are with your children for many hours doing the routine tasks. This is ten minutes of total absorbtion with your child. Talk about school as soon as they come home, or as soon as you return from work. Read with them, watch television together, play together of make crafts. Remember, if the child feels your total attention, not much more time will be demanded of you.

8. Read Chapter Six "Stress Management in the Home."

This will give you a few more ideas on how to deal with common daily issues and stressors.

We have focused on balancing home and work. We recognize the issues and may not have dealt with all of them, but we know that there are some things than can be done to decrease the pressures of working in and outside of the home. Keep in mind the positives about the situation rather than the negatives. Focus on the greater feeling of independence and freedom. Men, remember that working outside of the home gives the spouse a greater feeling of self-esteem, independence and freedom. This should not be seen as threatening but rather as giving you a stronger support for your own life and for that of the family. When both spouses work there is greater opportunity for social contacts, increased financial freedom and the satisfaction of learning new skills. Share the load at home. Take twenty minutes each day to relax. Make a careful plan of duties and responsibilities and remember that most women in the labour force work primarily because the family needs the money and secondarily for their own personal self-actualization. Go through the balancing act in those four life-quadrants.

What we have not yet dealt with in this chapter are the issues of single, widowed and divorced mothers who must work outside of the home to avoid poverty. These women have indeed greater stressors than those who have partners on whom to rely.

Single Parents and Coping with Stress

Statistics are certainly interesting but can never tell us everything. One statistic that is interesting is that approximately half the children and youth in the care of the Child Welfare System come from single-parent families. Single parents have fewer resources and support to assist them in the task of child rearing, and poverty can compound the stressors of raising a child alone. Single-parent families headed by women are particularly vulnerable to poverty. In 1990, 56 percent of such families were poor. According to this report, native children accounted for more than 20 percent of children in substitute care in Canada, even though they represented only 2 percent of all Canadian children. Canada's native people are the most economically disadvantaged group in the country. Experiencing multiple deprivations, native families often face greater burdens and difficulties in rearing children. The ideas suggested here will be helpful to all single parents and those who are economically deprived.

The Single Parents Plight

In our society a single parent often feels like an amputee. Something is missing, something that is needed to support life and limb. Although they are more accepted today than ever before, single parents feel the pressures of daily living to an extent twice that of reasonably happy married couples. It is not enoght that they carry the sole responsibility for themselves and their children, they usually also suffer great financial burdens. Upon return from work (if they do work outside of the home) the children's needs fall squarely on their shoulders. Often there is no one to share their burdens and their questions. They feel alone. Extened family members and good friends do help, of course, but this is often sporadic. The nights are long and lonely. The mind has time to wander over the valleys of the pain they suffer, causing long, sleepless nights. When they do get out of the house, they may feel singled out because many of those they meet have a spouse or partner to talk to and to lean on. Some people seem to lookat them with pity, but few make a move to assist them in their time of need. The stress is there.

The problem is not only in the preception of single parents. The community of married often do not know how to help. Men feel uneasy in approaching single women, wondering what their spouse might think. Women may try hard to involve single-parent women, but do so often without the support of their husbands.

The stress of single-parenting is further complicated by internal perceptions. Even though others may be able to provide companionship from time to time, single parents feel single, no matter the circumstance. They know their situation and they perceive others as literally singling them out as a needy adult. They do not want the pity but they perceive it, even when others do not think it. Thus, single parents tend to avoid many social occasions, fearing the stigma of singleness. Single parents have other added worries. They may feel the many days and nights of anger and depression, the feelings of loneliness at social occasions and the lack of shared rereation, but they also feel financial and economic pressures. Add to this the possible difficulties in the custody arrangements, the in-law interferences and the hostile ex-spouse, and you have a very stressful situation.

We recognize that there are good times as well; some single parents have learned to accept the situation and enjoy their aloneness. Many times the authors have had women come to them to suggest that being a single parent is not all negative. While this is true, we think that those women are in the minority. Yet, we want to recognize that some women have come to grips with their emotional and physical needs. They have reframed their status to an acceptable alternative. They have accepted whatever support has been given. They have involved themselves in community and church groups. They have sought out and developed significant friendships. Usually these are the single parents who have had enough money to make ends meet and have had suitable custody arrangements. Their children have had beneficial supoort of extended family, Uncles at Large, Big Brothers or Big Sisters. They feel productive, accepted, loved and self-supporting. They are truly the lucky ones. but what about the single parent who does not feel as good about the situation? The following suggestions have been shown by experience and research to assist in the plight of single parents. Some are easier to do than others, but in concert they serve to develop the life of the single parent into a relatively stress-free, or at least, stress-coping existence.

SEEK A NEW SELF IMAGE

A single parent feels amputated after the loss of a spouse through death, divorce or seperation. The roles the person once had have changed. The self-image has to change as well. If you see yourself as half the person you once were, you will also think of yourself as half a person--not complete. This image has to change. Seek to establish your own new image--the person you knew before the loss. See yourself as a whole person, the same loving and caring person you knew so well. Identify your inner sef by the person you are deep down inside and not by external forces. Do not try to bve two people. Children realize that one parent is gone and now you are trying to make up for it. Reward yourself often and frequently, seek others and tell them about your accomplishments for the day.

SET NEW GOALS

Following a loss experience, all future goals seem so distant and foggy. Some goals that you once set now do not seem to be realistic. You are now alone and the formula has to change. While the future may look somewhat uncertain, the issues are real. Who will take cae of you and the children? Where will you live? Where will the money come from? The path to self-renewal is not only in coping with the emotional loss, but the personal goal loss.

New plans have to be set. Look to those areas in your life that you set aside before the loss occurred. Set a plan into action to make small changes at first, followed eventually by bigger ones. Do those things that need to be done and then seek to develop personal goals. Take time to dream and imagine. Perhaps you are dreaming that you would like to move. Find out what you want to do and slowly set the plan into action. These goals are now yours and you will have much more energy and enthusiasm for them than ever before. It is a new life now. You have what it takes!

DEVELOP THE SOCIAL QUADRANT IN YOUR LIFE

To be able to remake your self-image and set new goals, a support system must be in place. Your children love you, even though they test your patience at times, but children can not meet all your social needs. The family and extended family you once had, may not be there for you now. Perhaps they are more of a burden than a blessing. The church you once felt apart of does not know how to relate to you now. Your co-workers may now see you as an 'easy mark' and try to take advantage of you. First and foremost, turn to your close friends. Remember, the support base may have changed but they should still be there for you. Some of them may have deserted you but others will side with you and those are the friends you want to turn to now.

You may have to look for new social relationships. While we were on the radio we recommended a Singles Resource Center because it is a wonderful support to many single parents. Do not give up on the community. Get involved in church activities, help in the nursery or in the eduation or music program in your church. If you do not belong to a church, then get involved in community service organizations or clubs. These are excellent places to find new friends because their motive is one of service and helping. Once these friendships are established, you can share your feelings with these new friends, hopefully they will be there for you when you need them.

If you work outside of the home, begin to develop new relationships as much as you have time or enery for. Seek out the most supportive, non-manipulative co-workers and plan some social activities together. Save some money for personal pleasures such as movies, dinner out, theatre, symphony or ballet. Utilize the interests that you may have once had but have put aside.

KEEP THE FAMILY FIRE BURNING

The bitterness that often accompanies seperation and divorce does little to build continued family support. Family members do tend to side with the biological family member, leaving you perhaps without the support you once had. Not only is this support lost, but the animosity and acrimony thrown your way makes your life more miserable and brings greater stress. Have a look at your family and extended family members and find those that are more empathic and helpful. Spend time with them and share your needs with them now. Seek to join in whenever the family gives you the opportunity. Even though this may be difficult for you, spend some of your time writing letters and making phone calls just to keep up contacts. Join in the family celebrations and keep your family informed of your plans and your needs. Ask to be invited over and do not hold back. Do not stay to long either because you need to develop other social networks besides the family. It is good for the children to receive all the family support they can. Do not be too proud--let the family members help you financially, if they can, without you loosing your own feeling of self-respect.

OBTAIN HELP FOR THE CHILDREN

Children can be the largest single blessing for parents. On the other hand, they also can be the source a constant frustration and fatique. To some degree it does depend on the age of the children, however, as they grow up they need your support more than ever before. Fortunately, as stated earlier, research supports the fact that single parents can quite adequately raise their children and meet their developmental needs.

The fact remains, however, that children benefit from the availability of both parents. There are destinct sex roles associated with maleness and femaleness. There are destinct differences as to how men, as apposed to women, nurture the intellectual, physical and socal needs in children. Although a single parent can try to be both father and mother, it is not an easy task. Try to take advantage of some of the other resources that may be available to you in your community. Utilize the support availible from your church and from the school.

School counsellors appreciate your request for help. Involve them. Visit them monthly if necessary and discuss your concerns. Counsellors can provide both individual and group counselling. They can assist the teacher in the classroom-related activities. They can also assist your children with school work, peer networking and they can provide a role model for your child or children. As mentioned earlier, there may be clubs or organizations such as Uncles at Large, Big Brother or Big Sisters that can be of assistance to your children.

Children feel your stengths and weaknesses. You are a mirror to their emotions. Try not to overprotect or smother them. Be as positive as possible and remain neutral in your comments about certain family members, especially about your ex-spouse. Your thoughts may be, "He never helps with the children. He harasses me. He doesn't keep his word or his promises." It is ok to think this to yourself, however, you should try not to say this outloud to the children. Be honest about your own emotional needs. Maybe your ex-spouse can be of greater support to you if he is willing and if you give him the chance.

Remember that little boys do become "daddy" when the father no longer lives in the home, and little girls become "mommy" when the mother no longer lives at home. This is all fine and good until you bring a new 'friend' on the scene. The more the children have become a support to you personally, they more they will react negatively to your new 'friend.' While it is good to be direct and open with them, keep a gentle distance and let the children be just that--children.

How Can We Help Single Parents?

We, who have not experienced the plight and problems of single-parenting, can only guess what it must be like. This author has been a single parent but is now remarried. This personal experience has deepened my understanding and given my professional work far greater focus and practicality.

Our society is based on dual relationships. Tables are set for two in restaurants. Tax benefits accrue to the married. Church pews are built for families. Family expenses often need two incomes. Schools count on both parents to support them. Banks will give the married spouse greater access to funds. Credit card companies often require dual incomes for security. So what can we do? First, we can sure try to understand the situation a little bit better from the other person's point of view. Single-parents include both the elderly and the young, the divorced and the separated and those who are bereaved. We have tried to give you a few ideas as to how single parents feel. But now we want to suggest a few things that we can do to help.

Take Time to Notice

Have you ever noticed that those who have experienced a loss, separation or divorce are more willing to assist others in a similar situation? The reasons are self-evident. An experience of loss sensitizes them to the feelings and needs of others who are going through it themselves. Our own crises sensitize us to the crises of others.

We are all busy people. The truly happy people are those who "love their neighbour as themselves." Caring about others as much as caring about yourself is truly the way to personal self-fulfilment and self-awareness. So think more often about the plight of single parents and take the time to help them. Help may involve financial support, social outings with a group or an individual friendship. Make a point of seeking them out just to say "hello." Sit with them at a meeting or church. Give them a hug. Just by taking the time to notice, you can lighten their load. Single parents often feel as if they have leprosy! It does not take much time to notice. It is a good way to begin.

Go the Extra Mile

It may disrupt your family life to invite a single, separated, widowed or divorced person into your home. It takes time and energy. You worry about what to say, where to sit and how much time this will all take. It costs you money, let alone psychological energy. Yet, to be truly helpful you have to go the extra mile. Take into consideration the fact that the single parent feels the same hesitation you do. They do not like to be singled out nor sacrificed as a lamb on your alter of 'doing good.' No, you have to be truly caring and interested in them. The extra mile is not as long as you might think. It could be a simple act of helping them with their needs by fixing their porch, playing with their children, babysitting when necessary, driving their children to school or simply inviting them to your home for coffee or dinner. Now you can move on to an even 'longer mile.'

Listening Without Evaluation

Single parents do not need moral or spiritual lessons at this time in their life. Some already feel full of self-recrimination, self-doubt and guilt. Single parents do know what to do, but may not have the resources or a friend to share their insights. They need you to be there, to care, to be interested and to listen. So sit down and listen. Do not interrupt when they talk. Show interest and keep eye contact. Cry and laugh with them. Be yourself. You are not a therapist but a listening friend and if they want advice they will ask for it. If they do not want to open up and talk, do not pry. Simply listen without evaluation. Show you care about them and show that you enjoy their company and tell them so.

Support Single-Parent Activities

While our communities do have agencies and resources, single parents enjoy the company of the married in order to feel more accepted as well as integrated into our society. Many single parents do not wish to be singled out and herded, as it were, to these 'special functions.' What we believe is needed is a greater integration of single parents into all activities. Yes, there is some room for special single-parent activities but the bulk of the time ought to be spent in integrating them into the community in which they live. That is why we need the sensitivity, the noticing and the walking of the extra mile. Many single parents do not attend 'single-parent groups' because they feel as if a 'quarantine' sign has been posted at the front entrance. You and I need to bring our families into the picture. Most of all, single parents want our respect and our love. To know we care is the greatest gift of all. This is true for everyone.

The great 17th century poet John Donne once wrote "No man is an island." No, we are not an island, but we can feel like one. Isolated from the mainland, with limited communication and only island resources, we feel all alone in the stressors of our daily living. This chapter focused on a way in which we can balance home and work for the married as well as single-parent families. While we have not been able to discuss all of the issues, we have highlighted a significant few. Balancing home and work is as difficult as it is to maintain a long-term stress-coping strategy. Our suggestions, borne out by experience and research, have been found to be useful in lessening the burden of working outside of the home and taking care of the family.

Chapter Six

STRESS MANAGEMENT IN THE HOME

Up to this point we have talked about stress-coping skills and techniques. Most of these also apply to the home. However, we want to discuss the home separately because the home is a special place with unique qualities. The home is like a hospital where you can go to recuperate and rest from serious illnesses. The home is like a restaurant where you can go in and freely order and select the foods that you wish. The home is also like a pub in which you can relax and enjoy good drink and discussion with friends. Most of us want to think of the home as a haven of rest. A place where we can let our hair down, be the person that we are. We expect our home to reflect everything that we are. We organize and design it in such a way that it is comfortable to us. This is as it should be. But when unwanted wars break out, the home can also be like a prison in which we feel trapped and lonely.

When the writers hosted a local radio program with daily interaction with the public, we had a guest on one of our shows, a writer by the name of Susan Brammer who wrote a book called **The Stressless Home**. Susan Brammer is a management consultant and a mother of six children living in the Berkeley area of California. Her book is quite a favourite one and should be purchased so you can read it in more detail. Some of the ideas in it are certainly relevant here. She said that the problems in the family and home are likely due to different patterns of personality, values and attitudes as well as stress reactions. She likened the home to a family business. A business is concerned about raising capital, increasing productivity, marketing, warehousing, having employees and accounting. In a business everybody has roles and goals which are negotiated and set forth clearly. The home she said, is much like this. The home requires a household chore system, a way of making the right decisions. The people in the home should recognize the different styles of thinking and reacting so as to contain the chaos. For Susan Brammer, the key phrase for developing a stress-free home is to find a way to establish goals and roles, with lots of compromising thrown in. There has to be give and take. On the next page, you will find a home quadrant exercise. Have a look at this system and take time to fill in as much detail under each of the six headings as you possibly can. This exercise should really be done with all the family members present so that the exact roles for each member can be worked out.

The Home Quadrant Exercise

Instructions:

Fill out the following questionnaire. Be as specific as you can in your responses.

1. The Family Goals

(Write down specific family priorities, goals and activities)

1. _____
2. _____
3. _____
4. _____
5. _____

2. The Communication System

(Who talks to whom about what? Who has which tasks?)

1. _____
2. _____
3. _____
4. _____
5. _____

3. Family Member Tasks

(Write down each member of the family and what they do or should do)

1. _____
2. _____
3. _____
4. _____
5. _____

4. Decision-Making Roles

(Who makes which decisions? Write down family and business decisions and who makes them)

1. _____
2. _____
3. _____
4. _____
5. _____

5. The Trust System

(Who is the confidant in the family? To whom do children go? To whom do you go?)

1. _____
2. _____
3. _____
4. _____
5. _____

6. Information System

(Who has responsibility to provide information, remind people, set dates, etc.)

1. _____
2. _____
3. _____
4. _____
5. _____

Reducing stress in the home requires a system in which everybody knows what to do and how to do it. This system could be called a Task System, A Decision System or a Goal System. Susan Brammer is right when she says that every home needs to take care of these areas if it is to function effectively. There can be happy homes, comfortable homes, loving homes, helpful homes, caring homes and teaching homes but each requires an immense amount of strategy and care. When these six systems are utilized, the home becomes a hospital where wounds are attended to and pains lessened. If one member of the family is ill, other people have to take over the roles and goals for that individual. Decisions have to be made and new tasks assigned. Somebody has to decide who is to communicate with the doctor or go get that prescription. The home as also a school where learning is expected, discipline is necessary and authority is respected. Like a school, a home is where rules are set and socializing takes place. Punishment is needed at times in a school and also in the home. Marks and grades are given in the school and people are ranked according to how they have achieved. The same holds true in the home. When you have set goals for your children and for yourself, you must find some way to evaluate whether or not those goals have been met. The school has a teacher who is in charge of the decision-making system and is clearly also responsible for the trust and information system. So clarify for yourself who is to make the decisions. Who is to be the confidant in the family? To whom do the children turn?

And then, the home is also a church where spirit and mind are developed, morals and values are placed in perspective and one learns to appeal to a higher authority. The home as a church is a place where universal values of worth are fostered. This is where your family learns to have faith in things unseen. Love in this setting is a resource for all to share. Spiritual nurturing in the home is dwindling today. You have to decide exactly how much of that is possible or relevant. Can you arrange your home this way?

Perhaps the home can never be entirely stress- free. We know it cannot. Nevertheless, if you know what to expect, you will not experience the same degree of anxiety and worry. Running a home takes commitment and caring, a love relationship that is continually nurtured, a willingness to learn, the ability to change and compromise and the nurturing of a tolerant spirit in values, attitudes, faith and morality. This is not an easy task but it is a necessary one.

The strategy that we have set out in the home quadrant exercise will be the first step in the prevention of stressors. Problems will come at you each day but if you have a system such as the one we suggest, it will be helpful. Susan Brammer is to be congratulated for her thoughtful comments. A home requires a balance in life style just the way each person's own life requires it. A home requires a balance of fun and work. You cannot be happy if someone is not doing their job nor if somebody is overloaded with too many roles. This system will keep the overload down. It should reduce the stressors that come to us when we finally arrive at home after a long day's work. The key is in defining and discussing goals and roles, utilizing each individual's strengths and talents. If someone in the family is good at managing finances, let that individual do it. If someone else is a good communicator, let them take on that role. We have seen many homes where people have taken turns, for example, in cooking. Although we think this is a reasonable idea, it sure can be a frustrating experience. One of the authors has used this system in his home. I will never forget how many times I had to eat raw potatoes and overdone vegetables or, indeed, burnt food with this system in place. Since we had decided on this system, it made sense to keep one's mouth shut since the people were performing their goals as set out and eventually they did become excellent cooks. Still, we think it is best if individuals in the home with certain gifts and talents do those assignments that they have the talent for.

People need to understand and prepare themselves for the multitude of roles in the family. There are always obstacles in a system of equal sharing of work, but this must be changed. Have another look at the home quadrant exercise and make a decision to get everybody together at a convenient time to discuss the exercise. Have a goal of improving the efficiency of the system in your home. Family meetings are a must and they really work!

Success With Conflict Management in the Home

It is never too late to learn ways to resolve conflicts. When a marriage is in serious disarray and conflict, it is not helpful to be benevolent, or so merciful that you would hold an umbrella over a duck in a rain shower! It is not helpful to forgive your spouse after you have exacted revenge. Marriage partners basically trust in each other. However, many of today's marriages have lost this sense of trust and commitment. Resolution of conflict is never an easy matter. It takes a will. It takes a belief in the purpose, value and sanctity of marriage. However, changing your marriage for the better is worth more than proving a thousand things wrong. It will not happen overnight. The exercises that we are about to present are just the beginning on a road to a healthy home.

Our relationships in the home are important and complex. We know that there are a few basic rules in conflict management. One rule is that we need to differentiate between what causes stress and what causes conflicts. Stress can be caused by customary anticipated events over children's discipline, stress on the job and bills piling up. Stress is also caused by unexpected life events: illness, death job loss, to name a few. Stress can be caused by progressive and accumulating events such as conflicts within the home, long term boredom with a career or job pressure. Finally, stress can be caused by personality and temperament conditions. The perfectionist, the wise guy, the jealous and the inadequate certainly can cause a lot of stress.

Conflict is another matter. The causes of conflict can be due to simple misunderstandings such as being late for an appointment or having mixed communication systems. Conflicts are caused by personality clashes where one person is too shy and the other one outgoing, or where one person is quite sensitive and the other lacks sensitivity. Conflicts are caused by poor performance in which we simply let each other down or in which we insult or abuse our partner. And finally, conflicts can be caused by differences in values and goals. Sometimes one spouse wants to work but the other is against it. This can cause conflict. At other times one spouse would like to go to church but the other spouse is against that. Conflicts over differences in values also occur in the area of saving and spending. One spouse may be 'tight' with money while the other spouse may spend too much. One partner, for example, may say, "My coat is ten years old, I would really like to get that new coat on sale." The other spouse may answer, "Forget it, we can't afford it." This type of conflict and lack of communication results in a power struggle that leads to anger and resentment.

There will always be conflicts. The point is not to try to eliminate them but manage them. The expectation in the presentation of the exercise is that we want to help you win in most situations without feeling that one partner has achieved power over the other which would increase the stress on the less powerful individual. It is not really in what you know but in what you do with what you know that counts in conflict management.

We are not all experts in communication skills, problem solving and learning techniques. However, all of us have at least a good dose of common sense. Our attitudes and skills in conflict management are shaped early in life. If we believe that there should not be any conflict, we are going to be in a constant crisis. If we believe that conflict is a naturally occurring event, perhaps even a daily occurring event, we will focus our attitude on how to cope. You may have been taught to 'button your lip,' or that 'fighting never solves anything,' or to 'turn the other cheek.' If so, you have learned to avoid, dislike or clam up, all of which are not helpful for any conflict management situation.

Before we begin with the eleven relationship building homework exercises, heed a reminder. It is a useful thing not to allow a problem to fester for too long before dealing with it openly. Deal with the problem just a little bit after the intense emotion of it has gone down so that you will not be as predisposed to yelling, shouting and insulting. In other words, 'cool off' before trying to discuss a solution to the problem. We usually say something we will regret when we talk while angry. Problems will come at us every day but if we focus on the issue with positiveness, we have a chance of solving them. Let us repeat. Stick to the issue. If the coat, for example, has caused conflict, talk about the coat, discuss your finances and future plans. Do not bring in unrelated issues such as, "Your sister gets a new coat every year. I always hated her. And I don't like your brother, either." This behaviour of piling high and deep is only good for farm yards, not for conflict resolution. What we want to focus on in the next few pages are eleven relationship building exercises that the authors have utilized in therapy sessions for the last several decades. We have them in large print so that they will stand out and be recognized and memorized. Have a look at these exercises now.

The Eleven Relationship Building Exercises

1 *Clear Talk of Needs and Feelings*

The first step in proper conflict management in the home is to learn to talk clearly about your needs and feelings. You will notice that this exercise asks you to use the "I" word instead of the "you" word. We know that it is helpful to learn this communication style. It is more helpful to use the "I" word in a sentence because the other person will not take offense as quickly. It reduces the emotion in a statement. It does not cause the other person to feel blamed. The "I" word allows you to state your feelings rather than suggest blame. The following examples may help:

"I get so frustrated whenever you come home late for supper."

"I am very tired and cannot do the dishes tonight."

"I felt jealous when you were dancing with that other person."

"I am really feeling quite depressed now. Maybe we can deal with this subject when I feel better."

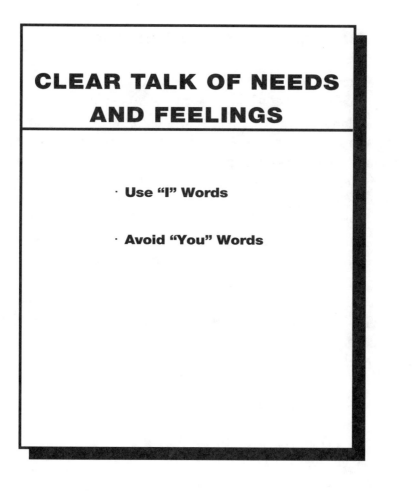

CLEAR TALK OF NEEDS AND FEELINGS

· Use "I" Words

· Avoid "You" Words

2   *Time-Limited InterCommunication*

Beginning with lesson #1, we move through communication styles. Have a look at the four ideas on time-limited intercommunication. It is necessary for couples to set aside at least one session every week for daily debriefing and clear communication of needs and feelings. Notice that the rules are to flip a coin to see who should go first and not to interrupt that person for at least five minutes. If one partner to is through in two or three minutes, that is fine, now the other partner can start. The task in learning how to communicate is really set forth in point #4, namely, to paraphrase what you think the other person has said. Paraphrasing simply means that you have listened to what the other person has said and now you try to say it back. Your partner then says, "Yes, that is what I meant" or "Not quite, I will explain a bit better." This exercise will help clear up a lot of hidden agendas and mixed communications.

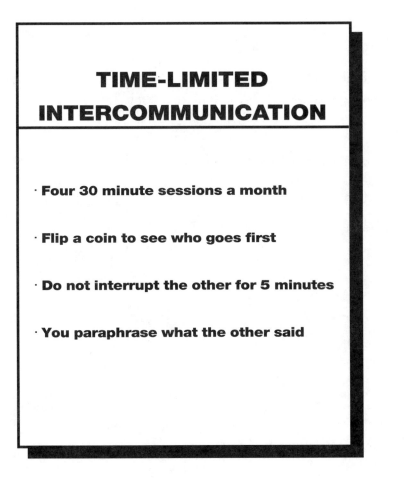

TIME-LIMITED INTERCOMMUNICATION

· **Four 30 minute sessions a month**

· **Flip a coin to see who goes first**

· **Do not interrupt the other for 5 minutes**

· **You paraphrase what the other said**

3 The Doctor Prescribes

We now prescribe different exercises, beginning with a night out, perhaps once every week. It does not have to be costly. This should be a time when there is no fighting and you simply enjoy. We find that when couples go to eat out in a comfortable restaurant, they are often more relaxed. We suggest that couples make it a point to go eat out in a lively and busy place where they cannot do any active squabbling.

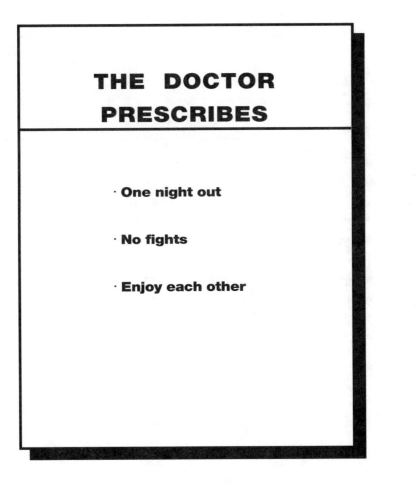

THE DOCTOR PRESCRIBES

· **One night out**

· **No fights**

· **Enjoy each other**

4 Make A Deal

This next exercise requires you to make a deal about activities. Many conflicts arise because one partner is off doing his or her own thing leaving the other partner alone. We are suggesting that perhaps 10 to 20% of all activities other than work ought to be independent, and 80% of this time should be spent in joint or common activities. This issue was really quite a surprise to us when we read in the literature that a common finding among all successful relationships was that of all the time that couples spend together on evenings and/or weekends, at least 87% of that time was spent together. Many spouses feel neglected by the independent activities of the other. Making a deal on doing things together but still allowing for some independence eases the conflict.

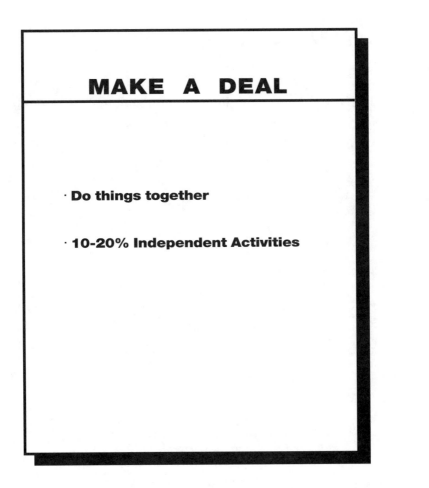

MAKE A DEAL

· **Do things together**

· **10-20% Independent Activities**

5 *Triple Increase*

Triple increase is a method where you both decide that the other partner can make specific requests of you. We give some examples for you to follow. While we suggest three specific things, it may be more helpful in certain homes to simply start with one specific request and then increase that to three once that is done successfully.

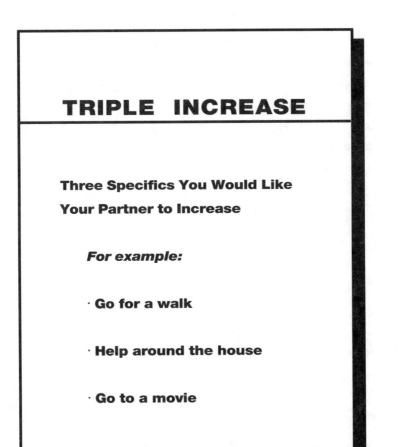

TRIPLE INCREASE

Three Specifics You Would Like Your Partner to Increase

For example:

· **Go for a walk**

· **Help around the house**

· **Go to a movie**

6 *After-Work Down-Time*

The next exercise reminds you to spend 30 minutes after work on down-time. This may be a time where you debrief on the day's activities and talk about evening needs. Naturally, clear talk of needs and feelings is necessary.

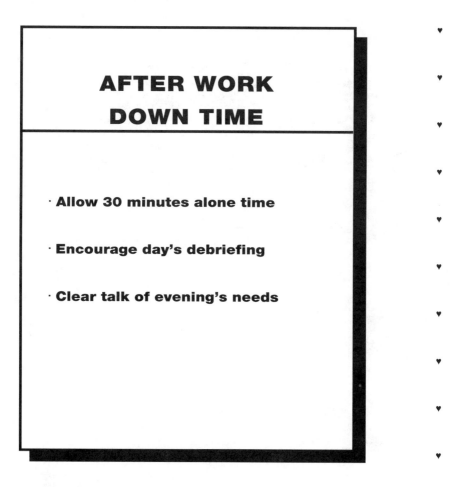

AFTER WORK
DOWN TIME

· **Allow 30 minutes alone time**

· **Encourage day's debriefing**

· **Clear talk of evening's needs**

7 Fighting Fair

The seven suggestions we have on fighting fair are very important in conflict management. How many times have you been in a fight where you lose sight of the original issue and bring everything but the kitchen sink into the conflict? Follow those 7 rules for fighting fair.

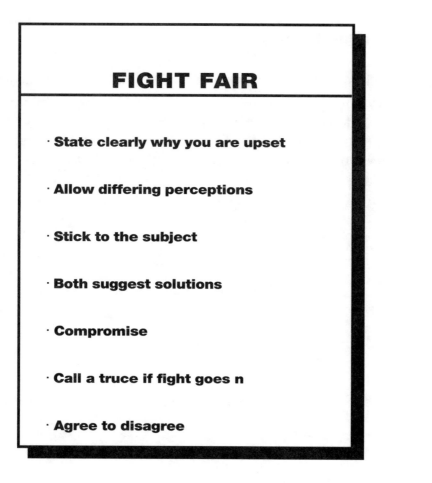

FIGHT FAIR

· **State clearly why you are upset**

· **Allow differing perceptions**

· **Stick to the subject**

· **Both suggest solutions**

· **Compromise**

· **Call a truce if fight goes n**

· **Agree to disagree**

8 Call a Truce

All of us engage in fights from time to time, even in the best of homes. There is a time when you have to call a truce. Agree to end the fighting but take turns giving in so that one person does not seem to be winning all the time. Remember that balancing the power is an important stress-coping as well as conflict management technique.

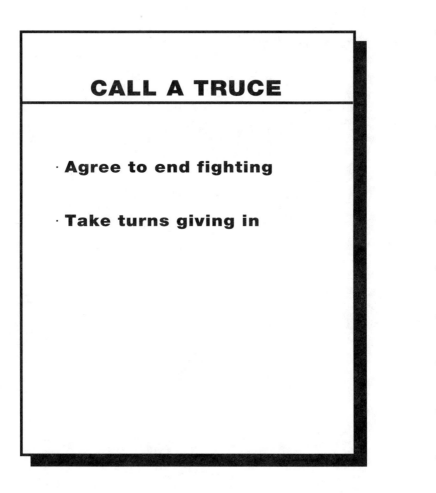

CALL A TRUCE

· **Agree to end fighting**

· **Take turns giving in**

9 Problem-Solving

We now move to problem-solving. Simply follow the five suggestions on this page as a technique in coming to grips with the problem before you.

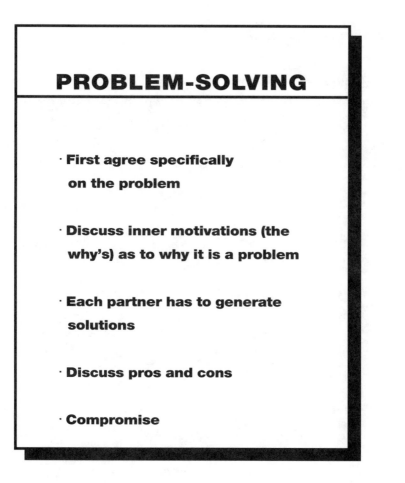

PROBLEM-SOLVING

· **First agree specifically on the problem**

· **Discuss inner motivations (the why's) as to why it is a problem**

· **Each partner has to generate solutions**

· **Discuss pros and cons**

· **Compromise**

10 Forgiveness

Forgiveness must be stated verbally and must be sincere. It is especially important for the person who has broken the trust to ask for this forgiveness and show some sincerity in doing so. The person who has broken the trust has the obligation to prove that they can be counted on and trusted again.

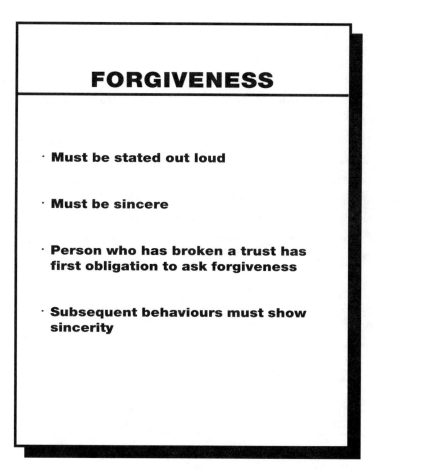

FORGIVENESS

· **Must be stated out loud**

· **Must be sincere**

· **Person who has broken a trust has first obligation to ask forgiveness**

· **Subsequent behaviours must show sincerity**

11 Sexuality

We end this exercise with a suggestion that sex and sexuality are an important part of the home. It is important for spouses to recognize that feelings must be right before one can even think about sex. There are things within the sexual partnership that vary from individual to individual but what is common is that feelings must be positive and preparation must be made for the sex experience. It is absolutely essential that spouses do not use withholding of sex as a weapon. People respond to the styles that make sex an enjoyable experience. We suggest that you take turns satisfying each other.

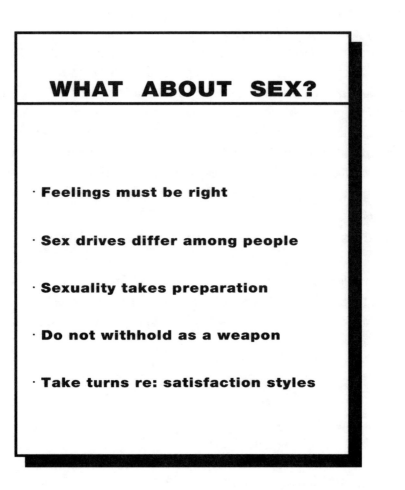

WHAT ABOUT SEX?

· **Feelings must be right**

· **Sex drives differ among people**

· **Sexuality takes preparation**

· **Do not withhold as a weapon**

· **Take turns re: satisfaction styles**

As therapists we know that settling conflict can not be done by talking to the partners separately. Problems and conflicts are usually caused in the interaction between people and so other individuals may have to be involved. Sometimes the whole family has to be involved. Our strategy for conflict management within the home is especially useful between spouses but it can be used by the children as well. Exercises can transform a relationship. It is true that when one individual in a relationship is caught in a power struggle, then these exercises will not help. While our strategies may look innocent, they are powerful and must be handled with care. They are designed so that you no longer need to read your partner's mind. They are built on the premise that real connections involve vulnerability and opening up to each other. Do not use 'power and control' over your partner. If you tried one of these exercises each week it would only take three months to see the benefits. Give it a try!

Success With Stress in Relationships

The old adage "Rough weather makes good timber" is not only hard to believe but also hard to understand when troubles hit. Many people live quiet, desperate lives thinking that this is their cross to bear. Destructive patterns in relationships are many. Here is a list of a few:
  - One partner feels out of love
  - There is evidence or suspicion of infidelity
  - One partner is dominant over the other --
  - One partner is never home
  - One partner is uncommunicative
  - There is jealousy in a first marriage or remarriage
  - Physical, sexual and emotional abuse is occurring
  - There is drug and alcohol abuse
  - The destructive process of unparalleled grieving is taking place
  - The destructive process of one partner being ill is taking place
  - A feeling is misunderstood --
  - One partner changes and the other does not

The issues listed above are just the beginning of a much longer possible list of destructive patterns in relationships. While many people believe that this is simply the way things have to be in life, it need not be. While you may experience the struggles and trials of life, you can still be a winner. It is possible to cope with traumatic life events like divorce, death, financial setback, job loss, major illness or a destructive relationship. In every obstacle there is an opportunity. It is possible to reverse destructive habits, destructive emotions and destructive thoughts. You can start by believing it is possible, and therefore, it is possible because you believe it. When you believe it is possible to reverse destructive patterns, you will be willing to do what it takes to bring about this change.

Begin by believing you are not alone in this. People all around you are encountering the same struggles, trials and vicissitudes of life. Begin by believing that you can move beyond being immobilized by tragedy and trauma and that you can use these crises to enrich your life. Begin by believing that you can grow through adversity. Begin by believing in thriving on another day rather than surviving one. What follows is just a small beginning of some of the principle strategies required to reverse destructive relationships.

Strategies to
Reverse Destructive Relationships

1. All relationships, like a garden, need continual care and maintenance.

Most of us like to putter around in the garden but know little about it. I am told that even the basic gardener knows certain rules about what vegetables to grow next to each other, so that they can thrive. The fact is that if you do not have any respect for a garden or do not care to garden, it will look like you do not care. Gardens need continual maintenance so that the vegetables and fruits in it can flourish. When I mentioned this particular issue to my colleague he said that this analogy reminded him more of the fact that one must seek knowledge of oneself before a relationship can grow. I would agree that you need to know a lot about yourself to make a relationship work. This means that the first step in reversing destructive relationships is to be open and honest with yourself and to fully explore all the needs, interests and attitudes that make up the core of your own being. It is hard to look at yourself. It is easier to see the good and bad in others. Remember the poem in the Introduction of this book? Practice to be truthful to yourself about yourself. Tough job! But it can be done. When you do this, you do not have to defend yourself all the time nor feel attacked, because you understand your own sense of self and therefore are not as sensitive to an 'attack' from your partner.

It is imperative that you consider your relationship as the most important thing in your life. The former treasurer of the United States currency, Katherine Ortega, said, "In the next year or so, my signature will appear on sixty billion dollars of U.S. currency. More important to me, however, is the signature that appears on my life - strong, proud, assertive handwriting of a loving father and mother." If you make relationships a priority, you will learn more about yourself and the continued need for care and maintenance.

2. Both partners have the responsibility to understand the other as fully as possible, or the individual's needs will not be met.

The second principle flows from the first. You need to know and understand yourself as well as the significant other in your life. Katherine Hepburn once said, "If you want to sacrifice the admiration of many men for the criticism of one, go ahead, get married." The good news in this rather cynical statement is that the person who really cares about you is the only one who really cares to criticize you. People who understand themselves and their partner are less likely to immediately take offense when things go wrong or when there are difficult times in a relationship. I think it is important for you to get to know the background, personality and defenses that your partner and you like to use. Blaming and sulking are bad defenses. Talking clearly about a problem is a good defense. It is important that you learn to accept each other's needs without judging each other. It is important to communicate honestly about your own needs and feelings so that your partner understands where you are coming from. Also, by understanding yourself, as well as the other person, you are far more likely to meet each other's needs.

Pope John Paul II once said in a sermon that to maintain a joyful family requires much from both the parents and the children. Each member of the family has to become, in a special way, a servant to the others. Service and servanthood are hallmarks of a positive relationship. But to be a servant you must know how to serve and you must know what needs are there to serve.

3. Partners in a positive relationship have to play together to stay together.

I think that the most interesting and astounding research data that I have read says that in a successful relationship partners have to spend as much as 80%

of their free time playing together. This suggests that in a successful relationship both partners need commonality in values, interests and goals as well as activities, at least to some degree. While it is just as important to allow individuality and autonomy to flourish, you have to be a friend to your partner and enjoy some of the same things together.

Common interests may include social activities. While you allow your partner his or her own hobbies and time alone, do not be critical of these. You may have to give in by joining in on some of your partner's activities, even though you may not be that interested in them at the outset. Nevertheless, it is important that you actually spend time playing together. Playfulness builds a sense of self, self-esteem, humour and interest in each other as separate, yet united people.

The story is told of a couple who lived in a third story apartment. Bad luck hit them: the husband was laid off from work for several months so that he could not pay the rent. The landlord evicted them. On the way down the stairs, he carried a television in one hand and a vacuum cleaner in the other. She had a lamp and the baby. At the bottom of the stairs she burst into laughter. The husband, who was not at all amused, said "Dear, this is no laughing matter." She replied "Yes, it is. This is the first time in 5 years we have gone out together."

Stories like this abound in our society.

4. In a successful relationship, partners have the responsibility to keep that relationship predictable and stable.

Success in a relationship does not come merely through finding the right mate but through being the right mate. Of course, there will be times when you will not enjoy always being responsible and positive. The mother who received the 1980 national Mother's Day Award said, "Of course I don't always enjoy being a mother. At those times my husband and I hole up somewhere in the wine country, eat, drink, make love and pretend we were born sterile and raise poodles." There are going to be many difficulties in a relationship, but it is an absolute necessity that both partners be able to count on each other. The fact is that most relationships cannot stand big surprises too often. So be as good as your word. Let your partner know you are trustworthy. Be courteous and advise about unpredictable events. Phone ahead and have enough respect for your partner to inform where you are or why you will be late, for example. Both partners must be able to know enough about each other to predict how the other will respond and feel in different situations. Stability is one of the most important aspects of life because it produces harmony and calmness.

There are other factors that are important when trying to keep a good relationship by reversing destructive behaviours. We have only touched on the most important aspects, but believe that the above statements are essential in both reversing current destructive relationships, and in building better relationships.

Questions and Answers

Improving Your Marriage

There is so much that we do not understand about marriage. It is like the fish in the fishbowl; he has little idea of the concept of the water that he lives in - water that keeps him alive! And so it is with marriages. We live in them, we know they are complex and we know they can and must be made better. Most modern marriages last an average of 9.4 years, according to statistics. The research also shows that 80% of all marriages have some serious relationship problems at some point. The "I do's" simply dissolve into "I don't", "I won't" or "I can't." Ambivalence towards each other and outright dislike for in-laws is believed to be the widespread cause. A recent Gallup poll found that men seemed more satisfied with their marriage than women; 61% of men still saw their marriage as the most important element in their lives. The interesting thing is that only 20% regarded having and raising children as the most satisfying part of their marriage. The majority report that their marriage had simply slowed down or grown lukewarm in the past fifteen years. Drug abuse, alcohol abuse and other serious physical and mental problems greatly affected some marriages. In most cases, however, there is simply a decline in mutual understanding and little time spent in nurturing the relationship.

There are two key issues that can improve your marriage. While these two are but scratching the surface of important things to do in a marriage, they are the factors that must be dealt with first.

Question:

We seem to have so many conflicts and problems each day. Is there a strategy or a way in which one can handle conflicts better?

Answer:

Conflicts are a common occurrence in every marriage and family. Expect it as the usual. This will help you understand that you are not dealing with a crisis situation all the time but that conflicts are a normal part of life and living. It is better to have the psychology, "I just can't wait to solve the next issue" rather than "Can't anything ever go smoothly?" It makes sense to have an agreed upon strategy for solving problems in the first place. When times are calm it is a good time to talk about the way in which you are both going to solve a problem. Therefore, the **first** thing that we would suggest is that you decide on the way in which you wish to solve the problem.

One way to start this process is to say,"The first thing that we are going to do is decide on what the problem is." You may be surprised to find out that the problem is viewed quite differently by your partner. So, to repeat, the first step in problem- solving is to agree on what the problem is.

The **second** step in problem-solving is to allow each partner five to ten minutes to speak to the problem. This is done by simply stating your concerns or points of view about the issue at hand. The **third** step is to both agree to generate suggestions or ideas on how this problem could possibly be worked out. Each partner builds a list of possibilities that may solve the problem.

The **fourth**, and final step, is to continue to talk through each alternative, throwing one out or adding another until you agree on the approach to try first. If this alternative does not work then move to your second suggestion.

While we have many problems or conflicts in life, and some problems may not be easily solved, it is important that we keep a cool head and a rational mind. The "fires of passion" lead to bad decisions. Remember, remain "cool." It makes sense that we continue to try different alternatives and not give up until we are reasonably happy. Keep in mind too, that sometimes compromise is the most important way to solve the problem. If any partner or spouse is too pigheaded, the problem may never get solved. It is not always easy to change your personality style; if you want to solve problems you may have to learn to give in.

Review the Conflict Resolution Summary Guide.

Conflict Resolution Summary Guide

Step 1.   **Use Clear Talk, without insults.**
Arrive at the Specific Nature of the Problem.

Step 2.   **Both Must Agree on the Problem.**

Step 3.   **Instead of Arguing over Details, Acknowledge the Feelings Associated with the Problem.**

Step 4.   **Ask What Can Be Done to Change the Thing(s) That Gave Rise to the Problem.**

Step 5.   **Discuss Alternatives as Calmly as Possible.**

Step 6.   **Reach Some Conclusions. Be Willing to Compromise.**

Step 7.   **Allow Feelings of Anger to Subside Before Asking For Intimacy.**

 Question:
My spouse always disagrees with me on how I discipline the children. What should we do when our spouse has such a different approach to child management and discipline?

Answer:
    This issue is complex. It makes sense that partners would agree, by constant discussion before the children ever arrived, as to who would handle the discipline and management. It makes sense that we talk about what approaches to take. While all of this makes sense, most couples do not seem to do it. I suggest

that in these circumstances we think about a good compromise. For example, if one partner prefers physical punishment and the other does not, agree on some reasonable compromise, which might include time out or withdrawal of privileges. Another compromise might be that a slap on the wrist or bum may be acceptable but no slapping or hitting the head. In solving this disagreement on child discipline, a solution may be to allow one partner to be the primary disciplinarian during the day. In this case, when the evening rolls around and both parents are present, the partner who has the responsibility for discipline takes the initiative while the other partner fully supports the disciplinary procedure. If children ever get the idea that parents disagree on how to discipline, they can manipulate the situation by misbehaving and then running to the parent who they know will side with them. Keeping a united front is very important. After the discipline has occurred and you still disagree with the method, then in private you can discuss alternatives in anticipation of the next time the situation arises.

Another way to try to solve this problem is simply to allow the other partner to take the responsibility for discipline. See how it works. This may be very painful for the parent who disagrees with their partner's approach, but it will determine the best method. It seems as if the differences here are tied to the way each parent was raised. We are now talking about value differences and these are the most difficult ones to change. That is, one partner may have been raised in a home where there was no arguing or fighting. This partner will therefore want a peaceful solution to a problem. This may not be how the other partner was raised, however, and this could cause conflict. Before discipline ever occurs, full discussion on which methods may be used is suggested. Draw up a list of the variety of ways you can discipline with full support from the other partner.

However, there are times when one must discipline immediately and swiftly. In such cases the other partner should not interfere or this could lead to a second problem in the marriage.

Coping With Loss

Question:

I have been going through a very difficult time lately. I've lost my husband through death, I can't seem to shake myself out of these feelings of depression. I don't even want to get up in the mornings. My family is getting worried because I can't seem to do the things that they expect of me. I feel down and I don't know what to do. How can I cope with this difficult loss? How can I get myself back to health again?

Answer:

The crises of life, conflicts, separations, divorces and deaths will always be with us. Bereavement is a natural process of working through the pain of a loss experience. We mourn not just loss through death, separation and divorce; we also mourn long periods of separation, loss of friends and family, loss of a job, retirement, the move to a new location, loss of pets, loss of the children's love and loss of innocence and health. The feelings, thoughts and processes are similar. The steps to recovery are essentially the same and how well an individual copes is a personal matter. Various factors can change the speed of your recovery: the depth of your love, the significance of the event or person, your temperament and personality and your physical and psychological health. Also, the extent and nature of the support of your family and friends is a very important factor.

Of great importance is the nature of your own faith and spiritual life. Individuals with a strong faith are able to cope with the loss experience of a loved one, for example, because they have the hope and faith that some day they will see that person again.

The symptoms are very common for those people who have experienced the loss of a loved one. Dr. Elizabeth Kubler-Ross has pointed out, in her very fine books, the stages of working through a loss experience. Take a look at these!

Denial

At this stage the individual cannot believe that this loss has really happened and often feels that it is not real. At this stage the individual may often think that the person will actually come back, and then sit up hours at night waiting for their return.

Anger

At this stage the individual will accept the reality of the loss but question God or doctors or others as to why it happened. Their anger is partially turned inward and partially outward. That is, they often feel angry and disappointed with themselves that they did not do or say the things they should have. Or, they feel angry at others for letting the loss happen.

Bargaining

At this stage they are making a deal with themselves, with God or with significant others that they will do certain things if only their loved one, who was their joy and happiness in life, will return. Often people decide to work hard for a cause or rededicate their life to something beneficial to themselves or others. Some people become volunteers, for example, so they can help others in need. Still others end up getting rid of all their bad habits to make sure that their body is clean and pure, and to help prevent their own death.

Depression

At this stage depression finally sets in because none of the above stages seem to be working. At this stage the real feeling of loss hits and the individual feels sad, lonely and miserable with floods of memories which may make them cry uncontrollably.

Acceptance

If the individual works through all of these stages, they finally come to the point of acceptance. At this stage they realize that the loss experience is a natural part of life, and they make plans for their own life and for the future.

Strategies for Coping with Loss

We would suggest these strategies be used on an individual basis to quicken the road to recovery.

1. Change the attitude toward the loss.

It is important that you stop "catastrophizing" the event. Stop thinking about how miserable you are and how lonely you feel. If you give in to these thoughts, it can drive you deeper and deeper into depression. It is normal to feel thoughts of self-blame or even those of blaming others, but if you continue with these thoughts, they will simply prolong the loss experience. Your attitude can either help or prolong the grief. When God calls somebody home, tell yourself it was their appointed time. We do not understand why people have to die. It is a hard thing to accept and nobody wants it to happen. But tell yourself that something good will come of this and that the loved one would have wanted you to go on living and loving as before.

2. Accept the feelings.

It is important for you not to fight the grief but to allow its expression. Recognize and accept the grief and express it openly. Cry, shout, get angry and feel yourself expressing the grief. Do not try to hide it from others. Let them know how miserable you feel. In the initial stages of bereavement try not to hold back. Let it show. This helps the body and the mind. However, you must be careful not to continue this show of expression for years. Expressing your grief for six months will be helpful. Expressing your grief for six years will be destructive to you and your loved ones.

3. Do not hide too long.

Give yourself alone time for as long as you feel you need it but do not hide too long. Get up and get out. Make a plan for the day. Do the best you can. You will find yourself fatiguing easily so take a break, relax and try to sleep. Expect that you will want to cry or talk about the grief. It does not hurt for you to talk openly about the loved one you lost. Good memories are always wonderful to share with others. Distract yourself. Put meaning into your life and fill that empty gap. Take long walks. Go to church. Visit friends. Get back to your job as soon as you possibly can. Since you are now able to express the grief outside of the home, you will find yourself being able to do some of your work and go home at night feeling very tired longing for sleep. Keep memorabilia for a while, but not too long.

We all want ways to respect and remember our loved ones, but if we keep memorabilia too long it strengthens and lengthens the grief. Put aside the memorabilia after about six months to a year. Pack these memories away in a safe spot for your grandchildren. But for a time after the loss, you can keep them around as a reminder of your respect. After a year on the other hand, it makes it easier for you if you make significant changes in your apartment or home so that you can begin a new life and a new you.

5. Accept support.

People do care. Let them give you support. Let them keep you company. However, it is important for you to tell them when you want to be alone. If possible, let them help around the house, do chores or just talk. If talking is too hard, just sit beside each other and watch television or independently read books. Do not try to put up a brave front. Be honest with them.

6. Find solace in your faith.

Let your faith move the mind and body. Faith in God, reading scripture and prayer can help you get back the hope that someday you will see this lost person again. Believe in the promises that are made through scripture. Accept this hope and repeat it to yourself daily.

7. Get back to a work plan as soon as possible.

Try to move yourself to a routine as quickly as possible. Force yourself to do it. Thinking on other matters will achieve a peace of mind, at least temporarily, and give you rest. So, get back to work. Work hard and work long hours. Get tired and sleep will come naturally to you at night.

8. Make new goals.

It is so important, after the loss of a loved one, to plan new goals for your new life ahead. It takes time and effort to think about what you would like to do. Nevertheless, within months of the loss experience, set new goals for your life. You will now have time on your hands, time that used to be spent with your loved one. If you do not fill this time and the emotional gaps you feel, you will be going over your memories again and again. You have to have new goals, therefore, to

break up the old patterns and old memories. As you begin to plan for new goals you will see joy stepping back into your life. After all, we
cannot have joy while sitting and thinking about our loss. Joy comes with living life to the fullest-- facing new people and new situations.

9. Seek professional help.

Sometimes, even after we have tried all these strategies, rest and relaxation still will not come. Depression is still there and you cannot seem to get yourself out of bed in the morning. Sleep is often hard to find. At this point, you feel that you need to get back to your work but you just cannot do it. Sometimes we do need professional care. See your family doctor first and explain the situation in as much detail as you can. Your family physician can refer you to a psychiatrist, psychologist, pastor or priest for professional help. Try not to see this as a personal weakness. It is really the intelligent choice if you recognize the need for help. Do not hide the need. Professionals respect you for seeking them out.

It will always be difficult to cope with loss. Your experience is no different from others who have had to experience bereavement and death. Remember, we will go through the same stages of loss. The road back to health, however, can be made more quickly if you attempt some of the suggestions listed above. Good luck!

Stress Management and Re-marriage

Circumstances for re-marriage vary from person to person. Some re-marry because of the death of a spouse while others re-marry because of divorce. Most re-marriages happen before the age of thirty-five, however, today many re-marriages occur after the mid-life crisis. Experiencing painful conflict sensitizes us to abuse and neglect. We become sensitive to even the slightest tinge of rejection.

Self-esteem becomes fragile. Individuals often seek out a partner with a similar background and we now have two people who are sensitive and fearful. Daily problems become unsolvable. Separation and a second divorce is much more common in this circumstance.

In most re-marriages, especially where children are involved, it is tough enough to get to know each other and adjust to each other's habits, attitudes, personality and special needs, let alone deal with the step-children.

Re-marriage has these additional issues to settle if there are children involved:

(1) children who resent the new spouse

(2) in-laws who might interfere

(3) ex in-laws who might still want access to the children

(4) different attitudes and values of the spouse

(5) jealousies over previous relationships

(6) lack of familiarity with each other's past experiences and friendships

(7) step-children who will not accept the rules of the new spouse

(8) different views on raising children

(9) different views on religion, sports and politics

(10) many other issues that need to be settled

Unfortunately, a spouse may have to choose between the love for the new spouse or siding with the children. It is more natural to side with the children because they are your flesh and blood and you are already bonded. This makes re-marriage a rocky bed on which to sleep. Unhappiness can result over little things that slowly pile up until they blow up! Each day brings about new issues, new problems and new insights. Once divorced, the chances of divorcing again are very high because the issues and problems in the first marriage were never really settled. Divorce hurts. It scars the person, damages the self-esteem and changes the person. It now takes even greater skill to make the new marriage work. What can you do? Here are a few ideas!

Strategies for Coping with Re-Marriage

1. Get to know your new partner very well before entering into co-habitation or marriage.

If at all possible, keep sex out of the new relationship until you really know each other well. Sex binds and complicates not only the present relationship but anything else that might happen in the future. Get to know the family background and personality of the person while you are falling in love. Meet the other family members. See how you feel about being around them. Spend hours talking to your new partner about personal issues, common attitudes and values as well as interests. Get to know each other's past by opening up as much as you can.

2. Upon re-marriage, the first priority is to work on your spousal relationship.

This means that you must present a united front for the children. Talk to the children about this and let them know exactly how you feel about each other and how you plan to handle the issues of parenting. The children must see the love and commitment between the two of you. Work on your own compatibility. Agree on a way to settle conflicts and disagreements. Without this, you have little chance of resolving any major issues.

3. Let each biological parent do the disciplining of their own children for at least the first two years of your marriage.

This depends on the age of the children. Young children, especially under the age of eight, will accept step-parenting discipline early whereas older children will be more resistant. If you are older and have young adults at home we suggest that if they are willing, you help them get into their own place. Give them some assistance and keep in contact with them weekly. This way, the daily issues, struggles and reactions to the step-parent will not arise and your own relationship will run much smoother. Biological parents must take the responsibility for administering the discipline to their children. If the new partner does this, the children will react negatively to whatever discipline your new spouse has to offer. If, after two years, your new spouse disciplines the children and you are in disagreement with the form of discipline used, bring this matter up for discussion at those times that you set aside to talk about these problems.

4. *You will need to accept a heavy dose of compromise or the marriage will slowly disintegrate.*

Re-marriage brings together people with different backgrounds and different upbringings. Household rules and duties will need to be shared and discussed fully. Bend a little. However, compromise is a two-way street. Both have to do it. Without compromise nothing can run smoothly in a marriage or home.

5. *Upon re-marriage start fresh by putting a new stamp on this relationship.*

If you keep the old habits and ways of doing things, they can become reminders of the past. Therefore, it may be necessary to move to a new home or apartment with new decorations. It may be important to change banks and even churches. Fewer jealousies arise and you can build on a new foundation. Start fresh!

6. *Build new memories.*

Your re-marriage requires putting past things behind you and moving on to a new and exciting future. What you once had has now changed. This change is often resisted, and causes problems in the relationship. When the relationship is not solid, the children will tend to react to this and cause more problems. You need to do many family things. Take trips and visit the museum, plan holidays and take pictures to start building those new memories.

7. *Give the spouse equal partnership and financial freedom within that partnership.*

What may seem like a small thing, like a joint banking account, is often a very big thing because it represents total acceptance and trust. Too many re-marriages are built on separation of funds, friends and interests. These marriages will last a few years because of companionship needs, but eventually they break up because the spouse who does not have the financial freedom begins to feel trapped. No one likes to come to their spouse all the time to ask for money. If both are bread winners and have equal access to the finances then this problem may not arise.

8. *Do not keep too many secrets.*

Perhaps some things are best kept quiet but lying to a direct question will cause guilt. If your secret is found out from someone else, it alone can break up the marriage. Open and honest sharing builds a new relationship and bonds it. If you do keep secrets, it will force unnecessary distance between you and your new spouse. Slowly, you begin to uncouple and separate emotionally. This issue should be discussed before the marriage and not after. A good marriage is an honest and open one in which all things are brought forward. Dr. Carl Rogers, the great psychotherapist, once said that "all that can be shared, must be shared with a spouse." The implication is that not everything can be shared. You have to have some discretion in terms of what secrets can be kept from a spouse.

9. Develop couples friendships.

New marriages begin with old friends and slowly new friends come onto the scene. It is always best that couples relate to other couples. Not that you would ignore old friends or single parents you once knew, but it is vital that both of you enjoy the social life of each other's friends. Sometimes this means developing new couple relationships. Marriages that last have an active social life wherein the largest part of that social life is visiting with other couples that you each enjoy.

10. Develop common interests.

This factor is seen as number one in building more intimacy in a new marriage. Research clearly supports this view. Couples must find activities during leisure time that both enjoy. It is not that everything must be done together, but many of the activities should be shared. This still allows for individual pleasures, hobbies and interests. In fact, you must allow for individual interests. Couples need some freedom and alone time, too! As a marriage ripens, couples tend to give each other more free time because the trust and love is there and the need to be together all the time is not as strong. However, strong marriages, as mentioned earlier, are those where the couple spends time together — especially in the beginnings of a re-marriage.

11. Hands off the children.

Step-children react very strongly to discipline, let alone harsh discipline from a step-parent. It is essential that the biological parent take prime responsibility for the discipline for the first few years, as stated before. Children do not take kindly to physical punishment or verbal abuse from step-parents, no matter what the age of the child. As important as discipline is, another significant issue in step-parenting is the need to refrain from touching, hugging and kissing step-children for at least the first two years of the new marriage, until the children are more closely bonded to you. Research suggests that step-parents keep their hands off and keep a distance until this bonding has occurred. These gestures of touching, hugging and kissing, although acceptable in a biological relationship, may cause misunderstandings and confusion in the step-children. Sometimes the step-children will make unusual demands for closeness and intimacy. It is best for the step-parent to back off and resist these advances. Instead, be liberal in your verbal praise. Spend hours in communication and play activities instead. This will help the step-child bond to the step-parent. Be generous to and not envious of the step-children. Be overly generous, in fact, so as to win their confidence and affection. Let the step-children keep some of their previous habits and roles, those that are neither unduly interfering nor obnoxious. Let the step-children have responsibilities that they had before the marriage. Make changes slowly and with full disclosure and discussion with step-children. Do not make any decisions affecting the step-children without consulting the biological parent first. Let the children come to you. It may take years, but the waiting is worth it!

12. Expect and believe in growth, change and self-understanding.

Men and women respect each other for their willingness to look inward, to examine the inner self and have a willingness to change. Women do not look to the size of a man's chest or his impressive accomplishments. I think it is also fair to say that today men do not look for external beauty in women, but internal strength. Today's research has shown that both sexes admire a person for the willingness to share, open up, communicate, be honest and be willing to grow and change. Self-examination is never easy but it is a necessary component of success in re-marriage. The psychology of self-examination includes thoughts such as, "Am I listening to my partner? Do I respect my partner? Am I on a power trip? Am I too controlling? Do I show respect to my in-laws? Am I jealous?" The 1990's is a decade of self-examination and self-growth. Re-marriage requires extensive self-examination on each partners' part. This willingness will result in a strong, healthy and beautiful new marriage.

We cannot deal fully with all the issues involved in re-marriage and step-parenting. Our book **That's Living, Too** (1989), has a major chapter on family concerns in which these issues are discussed more fully. This book, as well as the first book written by these authors, **That's Living**, is available in most local bookstores. A number of other books have been written for the purpose of giving people advice on step-parenting and remarriage. It does not hurt to get more information so you can decide if the problems you are experiencing are common or not.

Parenting, and husband/wife relationships will be successful if these relationships are nurtured in a fair, open and honest way. Be up-front about your personal needs and feelings. Relating to others in your home is much the same as making brand new friends. To have a friend, one must be a friend. This will require compromise, patience and a love for each other with a willingness to forgive the faults. Good luck with all of these strategies to help alleviate stress in the home.

Chapter Seven

STRESS MANAGEMENT AND OUR CHILDREN

Stress Management in Child Discipline

Parents wish nothing more than to have healthy and happy children. No parent wakes up in the morning thinking, "Today I'm going to yell, nag and shout at my children whenever possible." No, we wake up in the morning thinking that this is going to be another beautiful day.

Parenting is the most important thing we can do in this world. More people are parents than anything else, yet so little is done in our schools to help children in the massive undertaking of being a parent. In school, our children get over 1,600 hours of instruction in mathematics through grades 1 to 12, but only one hour is given to the analysis of human relationships. Some people say, "Well, mathematics is more important because it teaches you to think." We doubt that! Most people have an enormous hang-up about numbers and mathematics to the extent that it makes them feel deficient and even dumb. Others argue that parenting comes to us as an instinct. This is nonsense as well. We learn our parenting from the way we were raised. Parenting is not an instinct. Yet many parents feel that if animals can rear their young without learning, so can we. This is just not so. It is easy enough for robins to make the same type of nest and feed the same type of worms to their young. It is another thing to be a complex individual in an even more complex and changing world. Instincts sometimes do work for us but even the basics of getting food, clothing and shelter are quite complex in our society. Doing your best may be all you have got, but it may not be enough. Raising children is obviously a sober and serious business but it also can be quite a lot of fun. It all depends on the attitude we take.

Children are a resource and a blessing. Every child is equipped with a natural response for love yet the unwanted wars break out in the home. What can we do?

The traditional responsibilities of parents have been to:

MAINTAIN THE CHILDREN, that is, provide them with food, clothing, shelter, education and lots of love. This also means that we are to maintain our responsibilities for financial, social and psychological help.

EDUCATE AND BE A GOOD ROLE MODEL.
Children become much like us. As my Dad used to say, "The apple doesn't fall far from the tree trunk." As our children grow up we realize this very clearly. Children do what we do, say what we say and generally follow our example.

BE RESPONSIBLE TO LOVE THEM.
Some professionals think that love is an automatic thing. We feel that love, which includes pity and compassion, is something that we can learn. Training in love is as important as training yourself to be a successful homemaker or a good business man. Love does not necessarily mean that we give in to all of the children's requests. There are rules and there are consequences for rules.

EDUCATE SPIRITUALLY.
This is an old traditional value that has been lost in over half of homes today. This is a personal choice and you must make up your mind as to your responsibility in this area, but we feel it is an important factor to keep in mind. We must teach and act in a way that shows we know good from bad, right from wrong and the importance of giving rather than receiving.

DISCIPLINE.
This last responsibility is really an important one, and we want to focus on it in greater detail. To discipline means that we do not provoke our children but rather provide them with an example, without exasperating them by the way we communicate. We are to be an example, provide direct instruction and encourage our children as much as possible. Rules have to be set and consequences for the rules must be followed.

The first step in good parenting is to recognize that our children, the minute they are born, must conform to adult expectations in an adult world. Remember that when the baby left the womb he came into a cold, harsh reality. The womb for the infant was like a Garden of Eden. But even after birth our children's needs are usually taken care of. We feed them when they are hungry, we put them to sleep when they are tired, we give them a hug when they cry and we play with them when they are curious and playful. For the infant, this is a big, beautiful world to explore and to master. But then, into their world come the adults, the parents, and what do adults want of children? We say to them: learn to walk and talk, get along with sister or brother, accept responsibility, do your homework, stay away from bad friends, eat properly, be quiet, clean up the toys, eat the food when we tell you, stop playing when we say so, go to bed at a certain time, do not hit your brother or sister, kiss aunty or uncle, eat those vegetables, sit still, do not cry, get dressed, go to the bathroom, take a bath, clean up your room, get a haircut, study for your exams, listen to your teacher, do your homework, turn down the music!

This is an interesting list, isn't it? Children come into an adult world and we; often want to treat them like miniature adults. If we had the attitude that they can make mistakes just the way we do, our parenting would be much easier. Nevertheless, we do have to teach them how to cope with their changing world, their changing body and the changing family. We have the responsibility to train, teach, model and discipline.

While we ask our children to conform to different rules, they quickly begin thinking to themselves, "Mom has different rules than Dad. I saw somebody on television who acts differently than we do. How come they can do those things and I am not allowed? If it is ok to do on television, isn't it ok for me to do? My uncle talks differently than Dad does. My friend's mother does things differently than my mom does. I want to make my own decisions about what is best. What a confusing world!"

Effective Concepts in Discipline

Discipline helps teach children how to live useful lives and how to be happy with themselves and others:

1. Our guidance as parents needs to be based on trust and love instead of power and authority. Our job is not to break a child's will but to seek to shape and channel it through reinforcing those behaviours that are positive.

2. Children also need to be guided to learn self-discipline and preparation for their emancipation from the home. This is the ultimate goal of discipline. Our greatest gift to our children is to give them confidence and independence so they can explore the world.

3. Children make mistakes but we must still give our children responsibility. Children learn from our mistakes as well as from their own. Give them an opportunity to learn and be generous in forgiving their mistakes.

4. The timing of a suggestion to a child is as important as the suggestion itself. Effective discipline depends on knowing how to prevent trouble by proper timing. Being overly protective will just bring an intense reaction from a child. Therefore, seek a balance between strict authority and excessive leniency. Discipline when the misbehaviour occurs. Do not wait.

5. Helping a child accept feelings, and learn what feelings are, is an important aspect of discipline. Children mirror the emotions of their family, especially their parents. Putting labels to the feelings of a young child often reduces the fear and helps them reduce the intensity of their reaction.

6. Be sure your child knows that you understand how they feel because you have the same feelings. Good discipline means sharing your own world of emotions with them.

7. Parents need to feel good about themselves so that they can feel good about their children. Working on your own self-discipline is as important as disciplining the children. After all, "Do as I say, not as I do" is a bad rule.

Alternatives to Discipline

There are plenty of alternatives to spanking, yelling and nagging. Many books have been written on the subject. Remember that spanking may stop an action for a short time but hitting lowers self-esteem and teaches children to solve their problems through aggression. The following ideas may teach your child acceptable behaviours and not lower their self-image.

1. **Prevention** is a good rule in discipline for children under the age of three. Remove all those objects that are important to you so that they cannot break them. A person phoned in to our radio program asking for advice, "How can I stop my two year old from pulling the pictures, tapes and glassware from my living room sofa table?" The answer was, "Put them away or put them higher up." Distract them whenever they feel worried or frustrated and substitute another activity for them immediately. Removing the child from a certain room or circumstance is better than hitting the child. Praise the child for acceptable behaviour, and do not give attention for unacceptable behaviour.

2. Make a list of reinforcers. **Reinforcers** are those things that children enjoy. Reinforcers should be used to encourage your child's positive behaviours. Social reinforcers include hugs, kisses, words of praise and smiles. Non-social reinforcers include gold stars on a chart, having an ice cream with you or taking a trip to the zoo. Have a long list of reinforcers that you think will be encouraging to the child and whenever they do something that you enjoy and appreciate, give them a reinforcer. Make a chart and agree on a reinforcer. When you catch your children being good, automatically give them a reinforcer. To shape children away from bad behaviour to good behaviour, reinforcers should come seven or eight times an hour or even more frequently. Keeping charts on fridge doors for each child separately is an excellent way to discipline them.

3. Psychologists have discovered that using **time-out** works best for children from three to ten years of age. Explain to your children that time-out means time-out from reinforcers. Pick a room (or a chair in the corner) that will not provide any form of entertainment. Do not put the child in their bedroom because the bedroom should be a place to feel good, not a place used for

punishment and bad feelings. Be sure to remove breakables if the child is young. Get a timer and explain to the child when he is misbehaving that he will go into that room for a certain length of time. For very young children one to five minutes may be sufficient but for older children up to fifteen minutes has been used in the research. Set the timer and begin when the child is quiet in the room. Be consistent each time the behaviour occurs. For a young child you may need to stand by the door.

4. Providing **logical consequences** is a method effective for all ages. For every act there should be a consequence. We learn by our consequences. For example, if your child forgets his lunch, he will go hungry. When your child runs into the street, you cannot let him get hit by a car so an effective logical consequence is to place him in a confined area to play in until he learns not to go into the street. Be sure the consequence is linked to the act. If a child has broken a window, let him help you fix or replace it. If a child has spent your money, let him earn it back by doing chores around the house until it is repaid. Forgetting his lunch, or doing chores to replace an object that was broken, becomes his or her problem, not yours.

5. **Privileges and responsibilities** are more effective with older children. Discuss the privileges that you share in the family: privileges of love, food, shelter, etc. Discuss with each family member what responsibilities are necessary to make the family run smoothly. You can follow the Home Exercise quadrant that was mentioned earlier in the book. When responsibilities are not met, privileges are taken away. Do not make the removal of a privilege unreasonable. One night or weekend at home may just be enough. Older children can often decide what privilege to remove, thus taking the responsibility away from you. Removal of privileges is an effective negative reinforcer that works to shape behaviour.

6. **Use compromise** whenever possible.
    Do not think of child management as a win or lose situation. Because of peer pressure, children will put all kinds of pressure on their parents for certain clothes or activities. These are the times for you to use compromise and reach it through communication and discussion. Have children set out three or four alternatives and then you pick one that seems logical.

7. **Stay until obey**. This is a proper rule for children up to the pre-teen years. We have found it effective even for twelve and thirteen year olds. When you ask them to do something and they tend to ignore you, stay there, repeat the rule until they get up and do what you have asked them to do. Of course, what you have asked them to do should be reasonable. Stay until they have finished and then assign them another task or let them play.

8. **Communication** skills are effective for all ages. The way we talk to our children can prevent or lead to discipline problems. Communication of differences is important. There are differences among our children and we should accept that. Avoid encouraging competition or making comparisons between siblings. Understand that each child develops at their own rate, and this rate may be very different for each child. Always give a child a few minutes before changing activities. Make your suggestions effective by your body presence. Yelling from another room has never been found to be effective.

Sibling Rivalry

What can parents do to prevent quarrels? Disagreements amongst siblings is normal if all children in the family are raised as individuals. Basically, children need to learn to settle their own disagreements within the guideline of not hurting themselves or others. But there are certain things that you can do to help them solve their problems and prevent quarrels:

Strategies on How to Prevent Sibling Rivalry

1. Every child needs a few things that he does not have to share. Let each of the siblings know exactly what these things are to avoid unnecessary quarrels. All the other items around the house should be shared.

2. Children do need space for themselves, so allow them this privacy.

3. Each child needs to have a positive addiction. As much as possible, find that positive addiction and encourage them to have fun at it. For some children,

the positive addiction may be horseback riding, skating, playing the piano or mountain biking, and for others it may be drawing, photography or reading. Whatever it is, encourage it and spend some of your money in developing it.

4.   Children need to have some time alone with each parent. Alone time is probably one of the most effective preventive measures in child management. Each parent should set aside special quality time for being alone with each child in the family. This time could be spent going fishing, going to the hockey game or even shopping together. The activity does not matter as much as the alone time that you have with that one child.

5.   Try not to interfere in quarrels unless there is an immediate danger to a child. Teach your children how to solve their own disagreements. Take time to explain to them how the other person feels.

6.   Suggest a change in activity if irritability mounts up. Children need to vent their emotions just the way you and I do. Do not shout back at them when they yell. Simply listen and then redirect their attention to some other activity that each child can do alone, or peacefully together.

7.   Do not threaten your children by making your love conditional. A child should know that the parent will still love them even if they do bad things sometimes. A child may react by saying he or she does not love you, but do not take that seriously.

There are times when your children will come running to you to solve their problems. Try to stay out of this as much as possible. Do not always take the side of the crying child or the youngest, for that matter. Separate the children without taking sides and put them in time-out if they are hurting each other. Emotions are sometimes high when family members get home from work or school, so the best solution is to put each child in different areas of the home. They cannot fight when they are not together. Do not reinforce name-calling by bringing attention to it. Congratulate and praise the children every time they settle their own quarrels without name-calling. Help your children understand that disagreements are normal and that you have them too. Set a good example and your children will eventually come to model your behaviour. Remember, the concepts we have suggested are effective at all ages but they may need to be changed and modified as the children grow up.

Obviously we have not been able to deal with every circumstance. Use of any of these strategies, however, will reduce stress. Parenting really requires sensitivity, sensibility and sacrifice. And one last reminder: the best thing we can do for our children is to love our spouse and develop that relationship. In short, our children are unique and their experiences are always novel. This novelty brings about greater fear and anxiety which causes a reaction. As parents, our role is to uphold the goals that we have set for our family. Make the family a refuge from the often harsh world: an emotional sanctuary for everyone; a safe and nurturing environment; an environment crystallized in the rich imagery of love; a place of sharing lives, love, discipline, morals, attitudes and intimacy; and a place for spiritual growth, love and development.

Success with stress and family management would require all family members making themselves available to each other and communicating their needs and feelings to other family members. Family members that are considerate of each other, as they would be with their close friends, build a happy and healthy home. As parents we need to develop a family life with realistic expectations. There will always be disputes, but let us commit ourselves to working them out intelligently.

Develop reasonable family rules. A family cannot run smoothly unless everyone does their share. However, individual rights must also be respected. In short, each member of the family has to become, in a special way, the servant of the others. All family members must show concern, not only for themselves, but also for the lives, hopes and dreams of other members of the family. If the strategies that we have suggested are followed, the family will be the refuge, the haven, the support it was meant to be.

Managing Young Children

Small babies are quite wonderful. Most babies are born with the ability to communicate very effectively. We call this crying. When the baby cries we cuddle, feed, change, call for help, soothe or engage in some combination of these strategies. The point is that communication is instant and direct. The wise or intuitive parent can distinguish a pain cry from a hunger cry, so a child's needs can be met very quickly. As a baby grows physically and emotionally, the child is taught to postpone gratification and therefore slowly develops a sense of self. If communication ceases to be direct, problem situations are masked and will require detective skills for parents to assist in problem-solving. Let us talk about communication skills designed to enhance verbal expression and listening.

How often have you heard yourself saying, "Johnny, hang up your coat. Didn't you hear me, I said please hang up your coat. It is thrown in a heap in the middle of the floor. Look young man, I'm not fooling around, hang up your coat! HANG UP THAT COAT - NOW!" What we have here is a learning and teaching situation. I suspect many times tired parents will simply hang up the coat, because it is easier or just less hassle than trying to get the child to do it. Johnny is learning to wait until his parents are angry. He will have several chances to comply, in fact, this minor annoyance might just dissipate. When Johnny starts school, or kindergarten, or playschool, he is going to start with a disadvantage.

Diane, like most children, has learned to listen. When her teacher instructs the class, "take out your pencils" she does just that. John, on the other hand, continues his ongoing behaviour or waits for a definitive and perhaps angry directive. This is because he is used to this at home.

Young children can, and in fact must, be taught listening skills. This can be difficult, however, particularly if parents are not good listeners themselves. Some sound strategies are as follows:

Strategies to Teach your Young Child How to Listen

Step 1.   **Make sure the child is paying attention.**
                     It helps to consider and be sensitive to the child's needs and
                     interests. We can expect a better response if our timing is
                     appropriate.

Step 2. **State your request clearly, only ONCE.**

Use eye contact. Focus on the child so that the child understands that you are sincere and serious about the request.

Step 3. **Reward the youngster when the request is complied to, or at least when a sincere attempt is made.**

Step 4. **If the child does not respond, follow through by either taking the child to the task, or waiting for natural or logical consequences to occur.**

A consequence might be to start eating dinner without the child if the request was to come to the table.

Step 5. **Be consistent!**

Do not make many requests, hoping some will be honoured. Be simple and straight forward. Expect your child to respond and do not repeat instructions or nag, unless the child is genuinely confused.

These strategies work, they really do. The child who has been taught to listen has a distinct advantage in the early school years. Even very young children can be taught to listen if reinforced for this behaviour.

What about problem situations? Most families are aware of difficulties in children's developmental stages. We all know about the "Terrible Two's" and the "Frustrating Fours." Children need to learn about things like sharing and responsibility. These lessons often do not come easily. There will be negativity and refusal to sleep or there may be tantrums. New babies, or even new family pets, can be frustrations for young children. Jealousy which may include regressive behaviour, is not uncommon in this new situation. Regressive behaviour means that a toilet trained three year old will start to wet the bed. Or a five year old will start to baby talk. Children learn faster when they can model better or more appropriate behaviour. Children can be trying, and an adult temper tantrum might be therapeutic, but calm, firm, consistent behaviour produces better results. Let's look at some strategies for handling temper in young children.

Strategies for Handling Temper Tantrums

Step 1.   **Never allow this behaviour to succeed. Giving a child an ice cream cone to quiet her will ensure the behaviour reoccurs.**

Step 2.   **Isolate the child. If this behaviour is "attention getting" it is likely to subside if no one is there to pay attention.**

Step 3.   **Remain calm if possible. It is recognized that Murphy's Law applies here. "Your child is the only one misbehaving."**

Step 4.   **Reward the child when behaviour is more positive. Deal with tantrums quickly; children will continue actions which succeed, not those that fail.**

Sometimes children display aggressive behaviour that is so totally inappropriate that steps must be taken immediately to protect others. Sometimes young children bite, kick, break things or may even start fires. In these situations adults must be both firm and clear. "NO" is very appropriate. There must not be any doubt about the seriousness of the issue. Overelaboration and discussion with young children may be inappropriate strategies. Talking for half an hour about the dangers of playing with matches is not helpful in the face of danger. Nor is it helpful is the child is only two years old and cannot understand what you are talking about. If children recognize that their parents become very serious only in serious situations, authority is reinforced. The constant use of the word "no" in too many contexts can be confusing.

Communication is a two-way street. It is also important that we take time to listen to young children. Their ideas and concerns are important, and they need to be able to express them with full attention from the parent. All young children need affection, attention and acceptance. Providing this atmosphere in the home can prevent problems from developing. If communication patterns are open and honest during "fun times," the same patterns will emerge when problems occur and straight answers are required.

Communicating With Teenagers

I.   Communication Issues

1. Listen

It is important to understand the problems of a teenager before we try to solve them. Make sure to practice listening and understanding. It is pretty hard to understand teenagers sometimes, but let us try--they are worth it. By interjecting or asking questions, we may often focus the discussion around our needs, never finding out what was intended to be communicated.

2. When criticizing, attack the behaviour of the person, not the person.

Attack is a poor word, but the point is clear. You can focus on dumb behaviour, without implying that the person is stupid. We can help a child curtail snacks without calling him or her "fat." If children are told they are something enough times, it will eventually come to be believed.

3. Focus on positives and problem-solving as well as negatives and problems.

In turbulent years we often create the impression that life is one problem after another. Life would be so much easier if we could believe that it is one solution after another. Take time to look for positives and positive behaviour in your teenager. Comment on this behaviour often and it will reinforce the chances of the same behaviour occurring again.

II. Control Issues

1. Make few rules, leaving opportunity for much discussion, but the rules of the house should be firm and clear and apply to everyone.

Teenagers will challenge and test rules, so it should be clear that they can have input into decision-making. Some rules, though, are not negotiable and these should be clear and firm.

2. Consequences for misbehaviour must be logical and natural rather than artificial.

If a teenager returns the car later than promised, it makes sense that he or she should not have access to the car for a while. Missing a meal might result in a favourite dessert having been eaten by another family member. Logical and natural consequences are more effective than artificial means of control such as isolation or grounding for a period of time.

3. Separate large and small problems and focus on real issues, not petty misbehaviours.

Most teenagers do not keep tidy rooms. House rules might include efforts to keep untidiness out of sight and tidying periods to a minimum, but if small issues are raised day after day they can become overly important and parental authority is diminished.

A large problem that you and your family may have to deal with is if your teenage is taking drugs. Here are some suggestions on how to cope with this situation.

When Your Child Is On Drugs

One of the most heart-wrenching and difficult problems for parents to face is to learn that their child is on drugs. What we present in the next few pages are a few facts and figures as well as ideas on what to do and how to cope when you find out that your child is on drugs.

Young people today must make decisions about drugs that no previous generation has had to face. And this means that parents, too, must learn to cope with the reality of a world in which drugs are readily available to their children. One effective way to cope is to familiarize yourself with the drugs that are available to your children. All cities have drug and alcohol treatment programs. These programs provide reading material and offer lectures on drugs and alcohol. If you are concerned, then make use of these programs. Learn how and why drugs are used. Discover the dangers involved. Most importantly, this knowledge could open the door of communication between parent and child. Hopefully, these few pages will help your family understand more about drugs and help you answer your child's questions about them. While the government and law enforcement agencies have their place in trying to block drugs from coming into the country and arrest those involved, in the final analysis, it is the family that makes the difference.

DRUG USE FACTS

LIFETIME PREVALENCE	EVER USED
Marijuana/Hashish	50.2%
Cocaine	15.2%
Tranquilizers	10.9%
Alcohol	72.2%
Cigarettes	67.2%

* There is an increase in smoking in the 12-17 year age-group.
* Alberta teens who frequently use marijuana: less than 5%.
* Alberta teens who frequently use cocaine: less than 5%.
* Alberta teens who frequently use LSD: less than 5%.
* Alberta teens who regularly use marijuana: 2%. (age 16+)

The good news is that smoking has decreased to 26% from 55% twenty years ago. Alcohol use in Alberta has also declined steadily over the past ten years.

Why Do Young People Use Drugs?

☞ **Peer Pressure**   ☞ **Rebellion**

☞ **Pleasure**   ☞ **Anti-Social Personality**

☞ **Experimentation**   ☞ **High Reactivity**

☞ **Boredom**   ☞ **High Impulsivity**

☞ **Low Self-Esteem**   ☞ **Lack of Assertiveness**

☞ **Inability to Cope with Stress** ☞ **Maladjustment**

☞ **Escapism**   ☞ **High school drop-out**

☞ **Social Culture**

What Are The Signs of Drug Use?

General Characteristics

Changes in mood may include:
* weight loss
* uncleanliness
* trouble walking
* trouble talking
* too much sleeping
* red eyes

Changes in behaviour may include:
* skipping of classes--marks falling
* inability to keep a job
* money troubles, pawning things
* change in friends, will not bring them home
* trouble paying attention
* isolation from family, activities
* dropping of favourite activities or hobbies

CANNABIS	MARIJUANA	HASHISH	HASH OIL	COCAINE
air fresheners perfume candles incense (all to hide smell)	cig. papers plastic bags glass vials blenders	pipes blades alm. foil burnt knives burnt spoons	glass vials cig. papers toothpicks pop. sticks canisters	mirrors straws needles razors foil vials pipes spoons

Specific Characteristics

What To Do If You Suspect Drug Use?

* Talk to your child without anger
* Focus on their behaviours
* Set standards and follow through
* For now, do not ask why
* Ask for help
* Use communication skills
* Model positive parenting
* Use problem-solving strategies
* Parents help one another
* Explore drug prevention programs
* Seek spiritual help

What to do When They Come Home Stoned?

DO Remain calm

DO Talk to them and find out what they have taken

DO Call the doctor, if seriously ill

DO Tell them, "We WILL talk about this tomorrow"

DO Send them to bed and check them during the night

Do not SHOUT, ACCUSE then or HURT them!

What To Do The Next Day?

DO Talk to them immediately

DO Have them assume responsibility

DO Try to find out whom they were with

DO Let them know you will not accept their behaviour
     and that you will be watching them more closely.

Do Set up guidelines and curfews

Do Talk about other activities that are available instead
     of using drugs

Do not loose your temper!

Do not smoke or drink yourself!

The figures mentioned in Drug Use Facts were taken from Statistics Canada in the twelve to seventeen year old age group. We hope that you will find these facts and the suggestions in **What to Do** useful. Should you wish more information, please contact the Police Service in your area. Most police stations will have a Parent's Information Handbook on Drugs that they will readily make available to you. Remember, that most larger urban centres have telephone health lines. Health lines offer taped messages, anywhere from three to seven minutes long, that give information about alcohol and drug abuse topics. Take advantage of these resorces. Also,k the Royal Canadian Mounted Police usually have a Drug Awareness Co-ordinator that can be of great assistance to you under these circumstances. While the authors are not expers in drug therapy, we have found this information useful when talking to parents about the problem and then referring them to an expert who can work with the children.

Often the most difficult part for parents, in relation to the drug problem, is that the children are unwilling to go for help. When this is the case, we need to use a "tough love" approach. Rules have to be set and followed. The home has to be secrued with regards to valuables and money. Police may have to be called in or extended family members may have to help to take a child to the hospital. These are difficult decisions, indeed, but unless a tough approach is used, young people simply do not have the inner strength and resources to free themselves of this very difficult and life threatening habit.

The major risk factors for drug abuse in adolescents may be classified into three categories: behavioral, social and demographic. Consistently the strongest predictor of drug use has been past use--behavioral. Certain substances, specifically alcohol, tobacco and marijuana, have been shown to predate entry into other forms of drug use. Thus, parents have been quite right in decrying the legalization of marijuana since research articles from the Journal of Consulting and Clinical Psychology have shown that alcohol, cigarettes and marijuana certainly predate the use of stronger drugs. Socially, the strongest predictor has been use of drugs by adolescents, parents and friends.

The most consistent demographic predictors have been age and gender. That is, young males are most at risk for drug abuse. More complex risk factors are related to exposure to and interaction of all the risk factors combined, including poor academic achievement, anti-social behavior and parental drug and alcohol abuse. It is in the combination of these factors, rather than one or the other alone, that makes our children lmore predisposed to drug use.

Although most adolescents are not physiologically or psychologically addicted to drugs, the consequence of drug experiementation can be quite serious. The acute psychological effects of drug and alcohol use include: mood changes, impaired judgement and motor function, decreased attention span, memory loss and poor school performance. Unfortunately, the chronic physiological effects of drugs are: cancer, cirrhosis of the liver, and AIDS among the drug user population.

Prevention programs that emphasize physiological and psychological health consequences of drug use may not encourage abstinence even when effectively raising the consciousness of chronic outcomes. What is needed instead are primary prevention programs that are designed to discourage experimentation and especially regular drug use from occurring. These programs should be targeted at late childhood or early adolescence, which is usually the first risk period for drug use onset. It is the responsibility of the parents to emphasize healthy living behaviours such as those that we mentioned earlier in this book, including diet, exercise and stress reduction. We feel that in addition to home factors and school and family programs, mass media will probably show the most promise for increasing awareness and knowledge of prevention skills and, to a lesser extent, motivation to change behaviour. Mass media can make our children more aware and knowledgeable about drugs and can also motiviate them to change. It will depend on the extent to which mass media programs are complimented by other programs in the community, however.

The good news on drugs is that its wide spread use among the middle class is declining. Clearly, this trend caries a message of hope for us and for our families. Youth are increasingly returning to traditional values, as witnessed by their more conservative politics, increased interest in consumer goods, and greater willingness to make it through tradtional channels of business and professions.

While the above is true for middle class youth, lower socio-economic status and minority youth are experiencing a dangerous increase in drug abuse, dealing and violence. As substance abuse increasingly becomes an urban problem, we face an almost overwhelming challenge in our prevention efforts.

Our readings suggest a link between stress and drug use. Thus, it becomes even more important that we learn the stress-coping skills to avoid the impact of possible drug use in our home. Also, drug use in the home leads to family stress. Consistent and caring parents and teachers can lead to the acquisition of appropriate social competencies and will facilitate the development of hardy, resilient youth. This is so because hardy youth interpret threats as challenges, view their environment and stressors within their control and influence, and have a sense of personal commitment. Such youth perceive difficulties as less threatening and cope with stress more effectively than youth who may resort to drug abuse. We feel that drug abouse among young people is one of the greatest challenges of or time. While considerable research has already been directed toward studying the causes and correlates of drug use, much more needs to be done.

We hope that these few pages will have assisted you in a step towards alleviating this problems that you have encountered with your children. If you fear drug use, the stress management procudures will clearly decrease the possibility of drug use by ourselves as well as our children. We also believe in the premise that by helping parents to improve their own parenting skills, a protion of the psychological and social problems of their offspring may be prevented. It is assumed that educating parents about certain aspects of childhood and adolescent development, teaching them proper child-rearing principles and training them in effective strategies of coping with the various problems that they may face during the course of their parenting may serve to prevent or minimize certain psychological problems and/or social difficulties that might be manifested by their children. Thus, by reducing poor parent-child relationships, and by enhancing parents' abilities to raise their children properly, as well as to cope effectively with stress, an important, positive effect on the children's mental well-being can be determined.

Chapter Eight

STRESS MANAGEMENT THROUGH FANTASY

We all love babies. They come into the cold, harsh world with little ability to survive on their own. Parents are proud of their babies and worry about raising them properly so that they will grow up to be happy, independent and successful young men and women someday. This chapter is focused on the development of fantasy: its definition and its place in the rearing of the children that we brought into this world. First, however, let us focus on a definition and an understanding of what we mean by 'fantasy.'

What is Fantasy?

Fantasy, as defined in Webster's dictionary, refers to the unreal and romantic or the 'merely ideal.' Further definitions describe fantasy as a visionary approach, that is, being able to imagine in an extravagant and unrestrained way, so as to predict and foresee possibilities. Mozart fantasized his Sonatas and then wrote them down on paper. Fantasy also refers to the forming of mental images as can be seen more specifically in day-to-day daydreaming. Daydreams themselves can be a fulfilment of desires. How often do we daydream about having a special relationship, or even a new car or house. Daydreams are known to help children and adults work more efficiently, to overcome boredom, to be creative and to cope with daily living. In the world of fantasy and daydreams, a person is truly free. Fantasy has other definitions, such as the concept of hallucinations, where you are able to see or hear images and visions that nobody else can see or hear. While hallucinations are often relegated to the experiences of the mentally ill, they occur frequently in people but are under control. In East Asian countries, hallucinations are encouraged and taught as a way to cope with life. So while fantasy can be seen as a capricious and whimsical term, it can also be seen as an ingenious creation and an imaginative faculty. As Larry Niven once said, "Everything starts as somebody's dream."

Daydreaming and mind-wandering are both important and intriguing parts of a child's or an adult's life. Mind-wandering is perhaps the most obvious form of daydreaming. We regularly take brief side trips into our own imagination and memories even as we read or listen; occasionally these side trips can go on and on. Sometimes these trips are set off by sensations from the world around us, but often their origins seem completely internal. It is during these brief side trips, while accomplishing tasks that do not take all that much energy, that we can learn, rehearse or find a vision for the future. They are something that helps us cope with reality.

The development of fantasy in a child's life is very important from other points of view. In the book by Sher called **Wish Craft,** there is a quote by Vince Lombardi that is often heard at football games, namely, "get and stop 'em." This philosophy is certainly very prevalent in our society. It is important to get out there and get what you want even if you have to be aggressive and assaultive. What we are saying is that there is another way to get what you want. You must live your dream, use fantasy to visualize your dream-goals and wish that the best will come true. In this process you do not need mantras, hypnosis, super-human nerves of steel, excessive character building exercises or even new toothpaste. What you need is to simply forget the realities of where you are and say what you love.

Children are good at telling us what they love. Frequently they will ask us what our favourite colour is or what foods we like to eat. So when we use the word "fantasy," we are actually asking people to tell us what they love. Daydream and mind-wander. We are asking that through this process you search for your strengths and look for your gifts. Develop a map and a vision and then visualize a step-by-step process by which you can fulfil that vision.

Psychoneurobiochemeducation
(Psycho-neuro-bio-chem-education)

I remember reading an article when I was a graduate student at the University of Calgary. It was a paper delivered by Dr. David Kretch, Professor of Psychology at the University of California at Berkeley. He had given a talk by the very same title in which he hinted at the idea that if people learned how to combine their penchants for pills with their urge to find things out, then maybe they could develop a smart pill: a pill that makes us think and remember. Wouldn't it be a wonderful thing for parents, medical doctors and educators to have a pill that makes everyone smart.

In one of Dr. Kretch's experiments, which I feel has implications for our premise in this book, he tested the maze-learning ability of two quite different strains of mice. One of the strains of mice was particularly adept at maze-learning while the other strain was particularly stupid at the task. Some animals from each strain were injected with different doses of Metrozol after each daily learning trial to see whether there would be an improvement in their ability to retain what they learned in that trial. Some mice were not give Metrozol and the findings pleased everyone, presumably even the mice. With the optimal dosage of Metrozol, the chemically-treated mice were forty percent better in remembering their daily lessons than were their untreated brothers. Indeed, under Metrozol treatment, the hereditarily stupid mice were able to turn in better performances than their hereditarily superior, but untreated, colleagues. Here we have a chemical memory pill, which not only improves memory and learning, but serves to make all mice equal, whom God or genetics has created unequal. May I suggest that you begin to speculate what it could mean socially, educationally, politically and otherwise if we had drugs that would be similarly effective for human beings.

We have known for a long time that there are certain conditions that can make a "lame-brain" grow. What we are suggesting in this book, and certainly in this chapter, is that parents as well as educators, researchers and scientists of all disciplines look for exactly the right formula to help us grow and improve our situation. Educators certainly would welcome a memory pill but they themselves probably change brain structure and chemistry to a far greater degree in their daily interactions with students than we realize. An enriched environment can make a "lame-brain" grow. It is very important, therefore, that we look at aspects of developing children, their life, their world and their understanding, to create an environment that will turn dreams into reality and reduce the stressors in their life.

Children use daydreams, fantasy and mind-wandering frequently and so do adults. But for children it is a task that comes naturally and easily. We are suggesting that it is possible to turn this natural event into something productive and effective. Fantasy is not competitiveness but uniqueness. In fantasy, your assets become alive. In fantasy you see yourself as you want to be seen by others and by yourself. In fantasy you become your own biggest fan. What a boost to one's self-esteem! In fantasy we can analyze those things that we can or cannot do and then choose to do those things we can. In fantasy resides hope because in it we can see the next small step. By practising fantasy we can become a winner. It is important for us, therefore, to understand the growing child so that we can learn, and then teach, what children do automatically.

The Developing Child

Children experience the stressors of daily living as much as adults. Freud said that the biggest stress on an infant is the moment of birth. One can easily imagine how it must feel to be thrust out of a warm and totally supporting womb into a cold and antiseptic room with a doctor holding you upside down by your feet and slapping you on the bottom. What a great start to life!

In a study conducted by Dr. Yamamato, he asked nearly four hundred children to rate how much stress they felt under certain situations. It is clear that our children are under a lot of stress. The list that Dr. Yamamato produced, from highest to lowest stress, went as follows:

- Going blind
- Wetting your pants in class
- Being caught in theft
- Getting a poor report card
- Getting lost
- Moving to a new school
- Not making 100%
- Losing a game
- Giving a class report
- Losing your parents
- Failing in school
- Hearing your parents fight
- Being suspected of lying
- Being sent to the principal
- Being ridiculed in class
- Having a scary dream
- Being picked last for a team
- Going to the dentist
- Having a new baby sibling

While this is just a partial list, it does illustrate that children of all ages experience stress. Let us first look, however, at the development of young babies and children so that we can understand some of the factors that we need to know with respect to utilizing skills and techniques to better their life and help them become contented and happy individuals.

The Pre-School Child

The pre-school age group is probably the most studied of all age-groupings in child development. Pre-school children have not developed the guile and duplicity of school-age children, but wear their personality on their sleeve. These children's thoughts and emotions are quickly translated into utterances that eventually become words. Their behaviour is very colourful and transparent. For example, a pre-school child may run the length of the school corridor shouting, "Teacher, teacher." They may hug the teacher and say, "I love you." It is easy to observe but often difficult to understand. While at first speech and language development hinders thinking, words develop quite rapidly. It is said that in the early years, especially after age three, a child can learn fifteen to twenty new words each day. Researchers still do not understand exactly how this happens. It is also important to remember that by the time children are three years old, they have already reached half of their adult height. Since legs grow first and tend to grow faster than the rest of the body, children quickly learn how to walk and get around, which may create a difficult situation for most parents. By the time children reach the toddler age they have the ability to bend double at the waist, a feat that most adults envy. They ascend and descend stairs continuously, driving young parents crazy. These little children like to swoop and swirl, tumble and slide and flop instead of just ordinary walking or running. At the beginning of this age pre-school children, in many ways, resemble toddlers who love teddy bears, a frayed blanket and perhaps still use a pacifier. They hold on tightly to their security blanket, and have a tantrum if you put it in the wash. By the time these children reach five years of age we notice a tremendous change to sophistication, competence and self-assuredness.

Perhaps the greatest behavioral aspect of this age group is known as **behavioral contagion**. These young children, upon seeing someone else express an act or emotion, will copy the act or sound with great regularity. One can witness epidemics of telephoning and silliness. In quieter moments these children love to engage in conversation, but, like many adults, never seem to leave this stage and want to talk constantly.

There are other aspects of this young age group to which we should pay attention. Pre-school children have great capacity for sympathy, aggression and leadership. These children just love to soothe an unhappy parent or offer a toy to an ailing sibling or friend. They may burst into tears over the sign of distress in another, feeling what the other child is feeling. This is an act of **empathic participation**. Of course, some studies have pointed out that in these years the reactive sympathy comes from secondary motives such as feelings of superiority, guilt or anxiety. Often the pre-schooler comforts so that the other child will not tell on them or the pre-schooler may even laugh at a child in distress. This is not done out of maliciousness but because they do not understand the distress. What they see is an amusing spectacle.

Acts of aggression are usually exploration tendencies rather than passive hostility or outright rage. What may sound like aggression to us is merely role playing to them. Children will build on each other's ideas to surpass each fantasy in an outrageous style. Four-year olds are often heard to talk like this:

John: We'll cut his arms off.

Ellie: We'll saw off his legs.

Don: Let's hang him up in a tree and tickle him.

John: Let's poke him full of blue and black holes.

Ellie: Let's cut his hair off and put it in the sandbox.

At younger ages, pre-school children quarrel mainly over toys and possessions. After that, unprovoked physical attacks may begin. Later, social difficulties become the source of aggressiveness. The four-year old is already adept at teasing and fights begin with a slur on the child's character or competence. Most of the time aggression is seen in the language that these children readily pick up. Reading specialists already know that if we use emotionally-charged vocabulary like "Hell," "God Damn," children would learn to read a whole lot faster. Adult use of words in an outrage intensifies the use of that word for these children.

The Toddler Years

In the toddler years, play is the main source of activity and the way in which children cope with reality. For pre-school children, play takes on a very different character. Play becomes important to the point where the child makes a game of everything that is done. Even while urinating, boys will trace a curve or a line. While eating, children will turn a spoon handle into a shovel. There is real earnestness in the play. It is the child's way of experiencing life and learning how to cope. The child, however, recognizes play as distinct from the real world. Children's language and thinking give them new capacities for imagination. In fact, the main motif for play is one of daydreams, fantasy and dramatic role taking. Dramatic play is a way of learning and of being. It is a way in which children can make mistakes or even reverse a mistake and thereby survive. In many ways, the child's world in play reflects the adult's real world.

In the toddler stage, dreams are real events. Children may balk at sleeping in their own room because it contains too many dreams. They may insist on you sleeping with them or leaving a light on. One of our own children once remarked, "How can I see the things that are in my dream unless my eyes are open?" This is the extent of their thinking and understanding. Television has a tremendous effect on them. They will readily fantasize television events and dream about them in a distorted way. Magicians find pre-schoolers quite an unresponsive audience. This is because the pre-schooler finds nothing remarkable about sawing a woman in half, since in his own scheme of fantasy this is quite a possibility. Adults are far more entertained by **Alice in Wonderland** than the pre-schooler because the latter finds nothing remarkable in it. Even attempts to amuse a four-year old may backfire. For example, the father, on telling his boy about getting a flu shot, said not to try to run away. Because of this the child kicked and was seriously distressed. He assumed the reality of what his father said and experienced the agony in his own imaginary way.

One other thing about fantasies. It is during these early child development years that imaginary companions may appear. These companions are real and vivid to the child. The family often needs to adjust to the invisible friend.

As children get older their thinking is more in line with reality. They have greater difficulty in using fantasy to escape reality but it can still happen. Older children use language to order their world. They rely on past experiences and the reward or punishment of that experience to make decisions about what to do or what not to do. Older children have the ability to predict and to be able to make decisions about the future. By the time they are teenagers, they have a concept of time, a more differentiated self-image and an understanding of where life may lead them in the future.

The Role of Fantasy in Child Development

All children develop into unique individuals with their own minds, feelings and desires. While it is true that genetics gives them a basic nervous system type on the basis of which they will excite and extinguish quickly or slowly with the same stimulus, it is the importance of the environment that we wish to stress in this book. For example, some children become upset when they are introduced to a new person and have a difficult time settling down or extinguishing the upset state. Environment influences inner life and it is this inner life that affects how children view the outer world.

Children move quickly between reality and fantasy. Indeed, in the first eighteen months of life an infant is primarily driven by the satisfaction of urges and instincts. For example, if a child has the desire for food, a feeding instinct, that child may immediately start to cry. The child's psychology is, "I want to eat, now!" They live by the removal of discomfort and by the enjoyment of warmth and friendliness. At this stage, mother bonding and care- giving, as well as father nurturing, and love are the most important parts of that baby's life. It is at this stage, in the first eighteen months of life, that the blanket and teddy bear become a fantasy-image of the mother. Here we have the early development of fantasy in relation to the care-giver and in relation to a specific object like a blanket.

From eighteen months to three years of age young children are involved in toilet training, exploration of the outer world, and speech and language development. During this time they develop separateness from their care-giver. What is inside of them now comes outside in speech or in play acting. What was hidden becomes shared. They learn to regulate many of their behaviours and enjoy pleasurable sensations.

By age three they can substitute words for actions. It is known that during this time, fantasies diminish their anxieties when their wishes are at odds with their reality. They use their inner world to project their own feelings, to deny a misdemeanour or to visualize a very happy event. Their inner life and the mental activities that it represents serve to alleviate competing feelings like love and hate toward a friend or a care-giver. Their tolerance for frustration is still not developed and so they will express outwardly what they think and feel inwardly. Positive interactions at this stage are important in elevating and building their self-esteem.

From three to four years of age children develop gender identity and the physical and sexual sensations that go along with it. The boy will know that he is a boy and wants to play with boy toys like trucks and guns. The little girl experiences her gender identity by playing with her dolls and dressing up in Mommy's clothes. It is well known that during this time children are quite egotistical and narcissistic. The whole world seems to revolve around their feelings and thoughts. While parents are more concerned with developing their children's competence, this is the time when the child may struggle against outward discipline and thus, when they go to bed at night, they experience many nightmares and dreams. Their curiosity is legion and their fantasy is well-developed but curtailed by new words and forms of thinking.

During the four to six year range, young children develop a wider range of feelings and understand greater nuances of emotions. They can remember personal history. They realize that dreams and imagination come from within. It is during this time that they can understand cause and effect as well as time sequences. They know when they have to get up, when it's time for breakfast, lunch or dinner and they know what they have to do to be able to get ready for kindergarten or grade one. However, they are still quite regulated by previous and present fantasies. Their inner life is still vivid and their imagination is strong.

As young children grow up they have increasing capacity for reality testing. They experience life through day-to-day interaction. Development in children causes a greater facility for magical thinking but now they can integrate their wishes with their aims and goals. Young children love to daydream, use fantasy and work at pretend play. It is through fantasy that they can access their wishes and fulfil their needs. It is through daydreaming and mind- wandering that they resolve real problems in the world. Let us learn from our own childhood and our children. Reduce stress by daydreaming and by using fantasy. It is almost as if children are protected in fantasy from outer frustrations. Their inner life is quite rich with themes of love and hate, power and strength, rivalry and cooperativeness, good and bad. This rich inner life leads to decreased egocentricity and increased self-observation. Egocentricity means that the child is self-centered, feels as if no one else is important and feels that the world revolves around them. By the time they reach school age they can delay immediate gratification and see the world from the other person's point of view. Indeed, they can even share fantasies with other children and enjoy them tremendously.

By the time children reach seven to ten years old, school and learning become the most predominant things in their lives. It is during this time that their world is one of academic achievement, intellectual development and social skills learning. Social development and friendships are predominant during this age range. The world is now explored outside of the fences created by the family. Creativity, however, is still high and there is a re-emergence of aggressive fantasies. It is also during this time that we find increased nightmares, sleep problems and temper tantrums. Often, regression to an earlier age is used as a means whereby they can get love, care and attention. Fantasy is used to explore. This is probably the prelude to adult use of fantasy to escape reality. Exploration and mind-wandering, fantasy and daydreams are used to solve real life problems. Things are tried out in the mind before being acted it out in the real world. Life becomes less stressful because it has been rehearsed. While they are daydreaming they are certainly happy and contented.

During adolescence, fantasy life and the real world blend into one because of the strong idealism during the teen to young adult years. This blending of fantasy and reality is seen by their struggle for autonomy and separation from their parents. Peer pressure is very powerful. Their thinking is idealistic and they develop a sense of self through shifting their interests and ideals. The adolescent years are often described as the time of storm and stress. The inner turmoil is created as their idealism generates so many wishes which are translated into thoughts and language. Many of these expressed wishes are turned down by adults, creating excessive shifts in mood and emotions. Their intimacies are shared outside the family with a greater reliance on peers. Their physical body represents their real self and so they become highly vulnerable to publicity and television ads. Their self-consciousness and high sensitivity to self makes them more self-absorbed than ever before. Thus, adolescence brings a heightened attention to the inner world again. It is not uncommon for our teenagers to be staring right at us and yet their mind is far away. We often call them "space cadets" because they appear to be in a world of their own. During this mind- wandering, they analyze values, politics, sexuality, their own authenticity, religion and many other major issues in their life. Unfortunately, rules set out by parents, schools and society become barriers to their fantasies.

Fantasy as Seen by Eminent Scholars

Anna Freud was Sigmund Freud's daughter. She de-emphasized a child's fantasy life because she saw more value in direct observation of their speech and play. Nevertheless, Anna Freud and the great psychiatrist Heinz Hartmann saw the external world as being the primary shaper of a child's life. Both of them undervalued the unconscious mind and the fantasy life of children. Instead, they stressed a development of mental functions and importance of the child's family.

Melanie Klein was noted for her emphasis on the instinctual life of children. She believed it was shaped by the mother-child relationship and emphasized the inner life of infants. She saw the infants as shaping and actively organizing their inner experiences. To Dr. Klein, fantasies were very important in child development. Fantasy, she argued, was used to experience the world and organize the self. She believed so strongly in this that she would frequently regress adult patients in therapy to bring them back to a child-like state and gradually utilize their inner world of fantasy to recreate that individual into a new being. Dr. Klein saw the emergence and development of fantasy as something that should be nurtured and encouraged.

The great epistemologist and child psychologist John Piaget emphasized the role of symbolic play as a pre-cursor to the development of logic and orderly thinking in children. Piaget saw child-play as a behaviour that was not directly associated with meeting biological needs but was utilized to develop the inner being as well as the mind. Play allowed standards to be set by the players themselves. Play was not socially prescribed nor constrained by any social expectations. Thus, play involved the use and development of fantasy as an indirect way of meeting children's needs and nurturing their mental growth.

Fantasy in Adulthood

Fantasy, mind-wandering and daydreaming are seen to be important in child development and later in adulthood because they liberate adults and give them a time to relax, let go and create. It is a time for problem-solving. It is a time for mental rehearsal of the issues of the past and certainly of those of the future. Many adults have long since forgotten how to use fantasy and imagination to give power to their lives. While adults daydream, they do not do so productively. Thus, it is the intent in this chapter to show how we can use fantasy to liberate, solve problems and free us from the tyranny of reality. Fantasy allows adults to be liberated from duties and obligations but also to sustain hope. Jerome Bruner, the great educator at Harvard University, wrote of fantasy as "narrative thought." It is during times of mind-wandering, daydreaming and fantasy that Bruner experienced the realities of truth and life itself. He spoke of using fantasy to create "life-likeness," thereby experiencing the rich diversity of thought.

A child's imagination is but the pre-cursor of full- blown adult imagination. Without this development, adults would become handicapped in their thinking and emotional development. We all need to have the skill of generating fantasy for self-regulation and reality. Humans automatically assign meaning in organizing their experiences in the mind. We reconstruct life in our thoughts. We can experience even higher, or intense, emotions in our imagination. We are "wired up" to express these emotions and thoughts but control them where society says we should. We, as adults, continually block our thoughts, whether good or bad. Much of adult thought is to temporarily create a world where one controls, through replaying memories or through fantasy, one's outer life. Thus, fantasy as a form of mental rehearsal can be a great stress reliever. Think of the mental planning that you did before you had to give a speech, or a toast, or even before you asked a question at a public forum. We often protect ourselves from anticipated stress by anticipatory fantasies. As children, we acted out our thoughts and worries through play. We were aggressive and we usually won. By age three this ability is there in imaginative play. Even by the end of the second year a baby has learned words like, "No!", "Remember?", "pretend" and "dream." This is a tremendously important area of development for an adult to realize.

Imaginative play and the use of words in play are pre-cursors to eventual mental rehearsal and stress relief in adults. We did not realize the importance of imaginative play and words until we understood the research with autistic children, who are very deficient in play skills. Autistic children have less ability to express their behaviours and rationality because their inner world is all one of fantasy. Thus, it must be clear that we have to have a good blend and balance between fantasy and reality. Today, extended hours of television viewing have reduced our ability to fantasize and imagine. We have become reactive individuals . We look at television and react to what we see rather than using our own imagination.

Research has shown the incredible adaptive nature of imagination and fantasy in play for children because children who use it more often are more positive and experience less anger and aggression. High imagination in children also enhances their language and speech skills. It teaches them to verbalize aloud. Increased imagination and fantasy in children make them more persistent and give them greater sustained concentration, and also help them distinguish reality from the inner world. While they are better at play, they are also better at solving the real world problems. We know that abused children, for example, move into fantasy to escape reality. These are the children that often develop multiple personalities and eventually stay entirely in their fantasy world. Again we see the need for balance between fantasy and reality, but it is true that increased imagination and fantasy give children greater empathy. They can learn to take on different roles. Increased fantasy and imagination also gives children greater cooperation skills because they have learned to negotiate plots and roles. Leadership qualities in children are also developed because they can initiate new roles and functions. Children who have learned how to use imagination and fantasy are good readers and better story tellers. They can tolerate delay and defer gratification because play gradually becomes internalized inner thought. This inner thought and fantasy life allow them to sit longer when asked to do so and to tolerate waiting. This leads to eventual greater self-control and higher self-esteem.

The Development of Fantasy Skills

What fosters fantasy in play? Research has shown that attachment and bonding of a child to parents in early infancy is very important. Bonding is a pre-cursor to a productive imagination and fantasy life. Furthermore, we know that having a consistent care-giver is also very important since it relaxes a child enough to be able to move in and out of fantasy, thus creating the balance that we spoke about earlier. A parent's willingness to initiate play in games of fantasy and suggest plots, and to then step back so that the children can experience them as their own, is a wonderful task that builds creative imagination and fantasy.

Furthermore, parental storytelling and bedtime stories encourage the development of this unique and liberating skill. A family atmosphere of tolerance for floor play and a physical setting for the same allows children to have uninterrupted pretend games. This allows them to work through their daily stressors and frustrations. Overall, a sense of playfulness at home is necessary for the development of fantasy in children.

Great Men Who Utilized Fantasy

Many of the great leaders in this world who have been visionaries and productive thinkers were often abandoned as children or raised as orphans. The development and use of "fancy" and fantasy was what gave these leaders the freedom to grow and mature. Caution was not in evidence while they were in their fantasy world. They coped by mourning their losses through creative imagination, daydreaming and fantasy. Many recreated the past, linking the wish to the product. These great artists, musicians, sculptors, poets and scientists were able to express a wish in fantasy.

This is exactly what the great conductor Gustav Mahler said of his abilities and creativity. Mahler was a highly acclaimed musician and conductor. He stated that it was "his wish and fantasy to conduct a symphony and to write music." He saw fantasy as "a childhood replacement experience." Through fantasy came greater creativity and productivity. Recent studies in psychology by Dietrich and Shabad showed that the development of imagination and fantasy caused one to be inwardly curious, self-directed and able to escape the realities of the world without the corresponding anxiety. This capacity for fantasy allowed for the development of creativity and greatness. Dietrich and Shabad cite famous people like Charles Darwin, Louis Pasteur, Albert Einstein, Rudyard Kipling, Edgar Allen Poe, Aldus Huxley, Kierkegaard, Emmanual Kant and the great musician Mendelsohn as individuals who had developed this skill to be inwardly curious and self-directed while in their fantasy life.

Fantasy Can Be Verified by Research

In a wonderful book about children's dreams by David Foulkes (1982), he states "that it is not true that spontaneous fantasy cannot be studied following rigorous empirical methods." Foulkes gives scientific validity to the concept of fantasy and its development in children. While his book is about dreams and dreaming, he sees dreaming as "active imagining," just like a blind person can imagine visually. What is needed, he says, is a certain level of development of imagery and language. Even infants dream during rapid eye movement sleep. That capacity is there. Dreaming is the window of the fantasy life of children, clouded by difficulties in remembering. Through dreams we see a creative recombination of memories and knowledge. Pre-schoolers do not use dreams to fulfil everyday wishes but to express their world and the emotions in that world. Alfred Adler, a contemporary of Sigmund Freud, agreed that dreams were essentially continuous with one's waking behaviour. It was through the imagination of the dream world that one developed a style of life that helped to cope with the world and to relieve stress.

Another contemporary of Sigmund Freud's was Carl Jung. Jung saw dreams as serving to bring to the surface aspects of the total self that did not find expression in the waking self.

These writers were expressing another aspect of fantasy, namely that of dreams. We see fantasy as dreaming, but dreaming in a pre-conscious to conscious state. During times of mind-wandering and daydreaming we are quite able to answer the phone or get ourselves something to eat. Nevertheless, the acts of fantasy and imagination are similar to dreams. This creates another exciting possibility, namely that of the use of dreaming for creativity and problem-solving.

We Need An Environment That Creates Winners

Most of us never had or never will have an ideal environment. It was not anybody's fault. We are all human. It is true that if we are treated as a unique person with unique skills and told that often enough, we will develop enough security to withstand the ups and downs of life. It is important to recognize that children need to be disciplined, but also given the freedom to choose. Children need to be told that they can really be anything they want to be. It is important that we recognize the value of nurturing and love, as well as discipline for children. They need a great dose of encouragement to find out exactly what it is that they can or cannot do. So we need to stop blaming ourselves for the way things are and start using our fantasy to create new goals and new directions in our life. We are often so prone to complaining when things get rough. We feel like bailing out. But we must not. It is never too late to begin. Be careful, however, not to enter a fantasy that is simply living in the past. We do not want to get stuck there.

We disagree with Sigmund Freud that "the child is the father of the man." We have not really lost our best years because even in adulthood we can learn and encourage the development of fantasy and create a life of freedom and hope. That is, we can change and grow.

Begin by simply believing that children are given to us as precious gifts. It is true that sometimes we feel like moving away and not giving our forwarding address. We need to remember that children learn through love, care and consistent discipline. Children listen to us when we get angry with them without insulting them. Children pay attention when we meet them at eye level and talk to them in a gentle yet firm way. Children listen to us when we encourage their independence. We need a good dose of patience. Children listen when we praise them. We all understand that children are driven by the immediacy of the situation. We should not interrupt them when they talk nor evaluate what they do, but instead help them interpret their emotions by listening with the heart.

We create the development of imagination and fantasy if we play together with the children rather than lecturing them. We develop the capacity for creative imagination and fantasy when we are empathic, when we get into their world. This requires nothing more of us than to like them, be their friend and love them.

In this chapter we discussed the definition of fantasy, its value in our lives and its development in children. We have shown that many scientists and practitioners agree on the value of fantasy and creativity. To develop fantasy in ourselves and in our children, we need to develop a family system that has goals and roles that are reasonable. We need to develop a family system where there is agreement of how decisions are made and where trust and confidence pervades. We need to develop a family environment in which communication is clear and positive. When this happens, imagination and fantasy will develop automatically. Can you arrange to have your home this way? A good way to begin is simply to sit back, relax, close your eyes and let your imagination take over. Let your mind wander. Review your environment, your job, your marriage, your home and work. Visualize a new pathway for the future. Just go ahead and try this. See what happens!

BIBLIOGRAPHY

Azaroff, B.S. & Mayer, G.R. (1991). Behavior Analysis for Lasting Change. Holt, Rinehart & Winston: Toronto.

Azrin, N.H. & Besalel, V.A. (1979). A Parent's Guide to Bedwetting Control. Simon & Schuster.

Becker, W.C. (1971). Parents as Teachers - A Child Management Program. Research Press: Champaign, Illinois.

Beltz, S. (1971). How To Make Johnny Want To Obey. Prentice-Hall, Toronto.

Benet's Reader's Encyclopedia (3ed. Ed.) (1987). Harper & Row Publishers, New York (John Donne, 1572-1631, p. 267).

Blinder, B.J., Chaitin, B.F. & Goldstein, R.S. (Eds.) (1988). The Eating Disorders: Medical and Psychological Bases of Diagnosis and Treatment. PMA Publishing Corp.: New York.

Branden, N. (1983). Honoring the Self: The Psychology of Confidence and Respect. Bantam Books: New York, N.Y.

Brammer, S. (1988). The Stressless Home. Penguin Books: New York.

Brammer, L.M., Shostrom, E.L., & Abrego, P.J. (1989). Therapeutic Psychology: Fundamentals of Counseling and Psychotherapy. (5th Ed.) Prentice-Hall, New Jersey. (Carl Rogers. p. 24-35).

Briggs, Dorothy C. (1970). Your Child's Self-Esteem. The Key To His Life. Doubleday: New York, N.Y.

Brooks, Jane (1987). Process of Parenting. Mayfield Publishing Co.: Mountain View, CA.
Brunner, J.S. (1964). The Course of Cognitive Growth. American Psychologist, Vol. 19, 1-15.

Buie, J. (1989). School-based therapy aids children of divorce. American Psychological Association Monitor, Nov., 36-37.

Burka, J.B. & Yuen, L.M. (1983). Procrastination. Addison-Wesley: Don Mills, Ontario.

Carkhuff, R.R. (1985). Productive Program Development. Human Resources Development Press: Massachusetts.

Cartledge, G. & Milburn, J.F. (Eds.) (1980). <u>Teaching Social Skills to Children</u>. Pergamon Press: Willowdale, Ontario.

Corey, D. & Soloman, S. (1988). <u>Pain: Learning to Live Without It</u>. Macmillan of Canada: Toronto, Ontario.

Cramer, K.D. (1990). <u>Staying On Top When Your World Turns Upside Down: How To Triumph Over Trauma and Adversity</u>. Viking Penguin: N.Y.

Crook, M. (1988). <u>Every Parent's Guide To Understanding Teenagers and Suicide</u>. Self-Counsel Press: Toronto, Ontario.

De James, P.L. (1980). Effective parent/teacher/child relationships. In L. Hoban, <u>Mr. Pig and Family</u>. Harper Junior Books, New York, 34-36.

Dietrich, D.R. & Shabad, P.C. (Eds.) (1990). <u>The Problem of Loss and Mourning: Psychoanalytic Perspectives</u>. International Universities Press: Madison, Conn.

Dobson, J. (1989). <u>Preparing For Adolescence</u>. Regal Books: California.

Dodson, Fitzhugh (1978). <u>How To Discipline With Love</u>. NAL: New York, N.Y.

Dreikurs, R., Grunweld, B.B., Pepper, F.C. (1971). <u>Maintaining Sanity in the Classroom</u>. Harper & Row: New York, N.Y.

Dreikurs, R. & Grey, L. (1986). <u>A New Approach to Discipline: Logical Consequences</u>. Hawthorn Books: New York, N.Y.

Dreikurs, Rudolf & Stolz, Vicki (1987). <u>Children: The Challenge</u>. NAL/Penguin, Inc.: New York, N.Y.

Ecker, R.E. (1985). <u>The Stress Myth: Why The Pressures of Life Don't Have to Get You Down</u>. Intervarsity Press: Illinois.

Efron, C. (1984). Paternal deprivation - What does the research show? <u>Connecticut Association of School Psychologists Newsletter</u>, Fall, 26-27.

Efron, C. (1984). Children's reaction to divorce. <u>Connecticut Association of School Psychologists Newsletter</u>, Fall, 24-25.

Elkind, D. (1981). <u>The Hurried Child: Growing Up Too Fast Too Soon</u>. Addison-Wolsley: Don Mills, Ontario.

Figley, C.R. (Ed.) (1989). <u>Treating Stress in Families</u>. Brunner/Mazel: New York, N.Y.

Foulkes, D. (1982). <u>Children's Dreams</u>. Toronto: John Wiley.

Freedman, J. (1989). Happy People. Basic Books: New York.

Freud, A. (1986). The Ego and the Mechanisms of Defense. International Universities Press: New York.

Freud, A., & Donn, S. (1951). An Experiment in Group Upbringing in The Psychoanalytic Study of the Child, Vol. 6, 111-120.

Galambos, N.L., & Walters, B.J. (1992). Work Hours, Schedule Inflexibility, and Stress in Dual-Earner Spouses. Canadian Journal of Behavioral Science, Vol. 24(3), 290-302.

Ginott, Haim. (1971). Between Parent and Teenager. Avon: New York, N.Y.

Ginott, Haim. (1969). Between Parent and Child. Avon: New York, N.Y.

Glasser, William (1975). Schools Without Failure. Harper and Row: New York, N.Y.

Glasser, W. (1984). Control Theory: A New Explanation of How We Control Our Lives. Harper & Row: New York, N.Y.

Goldstein, J. & Soaves, M. (1972). The Joy Within: A Beginning Guide to Mediation. Prentice-Hall: New York, N.Y.

Gordon, Thomas (1970). Parent Effectiveness Training: The Tested New Way To Raise Responsible Children. McKay, Inc.: New York, N.Y.

Gredler, G.R. (1992). School Readings: Assessment and Educational Issues. Clinical Psychology Publishing Co.: Brandon.

Halpern, J. (1987). Helping Your Aging Parents: A Practical Guide for Adult Children. Fawcett Crest: New York, N.Y.

Hammill, D.D., Bartel, N.R. & Bunch, G.O. (1984). Teaching Children with Learning and Behavior Problems. (Canadian Edition). Allyn & Bacon: Toronto, Ontario.

Hanson, P. (1986). The Joy of Stress. Basic Books: Toronto.

Janzen, H., Paterson, J. & Blashko, C. (1989). That's Living, Too. Three Pears Publishing: Edmonton, Alberta.

Janzen, H., Paterson, J. & Blashko, C. (1989). That's Living. Three Pears Publishing: Edmonton, Alberta.

Johanson, S. (1988). Talk Sex. Penguin Books: New York, N.Y.

Kagen, J., Kearley, R., & Zelazo, P. (1978). Infancy: Its Place in Human Development. Harvard University Press: Boston.

Kaufman, G. (1989). The Psychology of Shame. Springer Publishing Company: New York, N.Y.

Klein, M. (1975). Envy and Gratitude and Other Works, 1946-1963. Hogarth: London.

Klinger, E. (1987). The Power of Daydreams. Psychology Today. (October), 37-44.

Koch, J. & Koch, L. (1976). The urgent drive to make good marriages better. Psychology Today, Sept., 33-38.

L'Abate, L. (1985). The Handbook of Family Psychology and Therapy, Vol. 1 & 2. Dorsey Press: Homewood, Illinois.

Lamb, M.F. (1981). The Role of the Father in Child Development, 2nd Ed.. John Wiley & Sons: Toronto, Ontario.

Lang, D. (1990). Family Harmony: Coping With Your Challenging Relatives. Prentice-Hall: Toronto, Ontario.

Lewis, M. (Ed.)(1991). Child and Adolescent Psychiatry. Baltimore: Williams and Wilkins.

Long, G.H. (1986). Occupational Stress, Health and Coping Strategies in Female Managers. Unpublished Ph.D. Dissertation, University of Alberta, Edmonton, Alberta.

McCubbin, H.I. & Figley, C.R. (1983). Stress and the Family (Vol. 1): Coping With Normative Transition. Brunner/Mazel: New York; N.Y.

McKee, M. (1988). How To Handle Stress. Great Quotations Inc: Lombard, Illinois.

Miller, T.W. (1989). Stressful Life Events. International University Press, Inc.: Madison, Conn.

Millon, T. (1981). Disorders of Personality: DSM-III, Axis II. John Wiley & Sons: Toronto.

Morrison, A.M., White, P.R. & Van Velson, E. (1987). Executive Women: Substance Plus Style. Psychology Today, August, 18-26.

Papolos, D.R. & Papolos, J. (1987). Overcoming Depression. Harper & Row: New York, N.Y.

Paterson, J. & Blashko, C., & Janzen, H. (1990). When You Stand Alone. Three Pears Publishing: Edmonton, Alberta.

Patterson, G.R. & Gullion, M.E. (1971). Living With Children. Research Press: Champaign, Illinois.

Peale, N.V. (1956). The Power of Positive Thinking. Fawcett Crest: New York.

Rainey, D. & Rainey, B. (1986). Building Your Mate's Self-Esteem. Here's Life Publishers: California.

Reichman, R. (1989). The Stranger in Your Bed. John Wiley: Toronto, Ontario.

Remley, A. (1988). The great parental value shift: From obedience to independence. Psychology Today, October, 56-59.

Reskies, E. (1987). Stress Management in the Healthy Type A. Guilford Press: London.

Richardson, L.A. (1983). Working Couples: How To Successfully Combine Family and Work. Self-Counsel Press: Toronto, Ontario.

Robertson, James & Robertson, Joyce (1983). Baby In The Family. Penguin: New York, N.Y. 10010.

Rogers, C.R. (1980). A Way of Being. Houghton Mifflin, N.Y.

Rosenthal, N.E., & Blehar, M.C. (1989). Seasonal Affective Disorders and Phototherapy. (Eds.) Guilford Press: New York.

Ross, D.P. & Shillington. (1989). The Canadian Fact Book on Poverty. Canadian Council on Social Development: Ottawa, Ontario.

Scarf, M. (1986). Intimate partners: Partners in love and marriage. The Atlantic Monthly, Dec., 66-76.

Selye, H. (Ed.) (1983). Selye's Guide to Stress Research, Vol. 2. Nostrand Reinhold: Toronto.

Sher, B. (1979). Wishcraft: How To Get What You Really Want. New York: Ballantine Books.

Smith, Judith M. & Smith, Donald, E. (1976). Child Management: A Program For Parents and Teachers. Res Press: Champaign, IL.

Tauris, C. (1975). Anger: The Misunderstood Emotion. Simon & Schuster: New York.

Tauris, C. (1975). How psychology short-changes mothers. Psychology Today, Sept., 10-11.

Tubesing, N.L. & Tubesing, D.A. (1988). Structured Exercises in Stress Management (Vols. 1, 2, 3, 4). Whole Person Press: Duluth, MN.

Vannicelli, M. (1992). Removing the Roadblocks: Group Psychotherapy With Substance Abusers and Family Members. Guilford Press: London.

Vaughn, D. (1986). Uncoupling: Turning Points in Intimate Relationships; Oxford Press: New York, N.Y.

Walker, G. (1985). <u>Second Wife, Second Best?</u> Doubleday: Markham, Ontario.

Walsh, M. (1990). <u>Emptying The Nest</u>. Prentice-Hall: Toronto.

Waring, E.M. (1988). <u>Enhancing Marital Intimacy Through Facilitating Cognitive Self-Disclosure</u>. Brunner/Mazel: New York, N.Y.

White, Burton, L. (1987). <u>First Three Years of Life</u>. Prentice Hall: Englewood Cliffs, N.J.

Wielkiewicz, R.M. (1986). <u>Behavior Management in the Schools</u>. Pergamon Press: Willowdale, Ontario.

Witkin-Lanoil, G. (1987). <u>The Male Stress Syndrome</u>. Berkley Books: New York, N.Y.

Witkin-Lanoil, G. (1986). <u>The Female Stress Syndrome</u>. Berkley Books: New York, N.Y.
Woolfolk, R.L. & Lenrer, P.M. (Eds.) (1984). <u>Principles and Practice of Stress Management</u>. Guilford Press: London.

Wycliff, J. & Unell, B.C. (1984). <u>Discipline Without Shouting or Spanking</u>. Meadowbrook Books: New York, N.Y.

Youngs, B.B. (1985). <u>Stress in Children</u>. Avon Books: New York, N.Y.

Swede, S. & Jaffe, S.S. (1987). <u>The Panic Attack Recovery Book</u>. New American Library: New York, N.Y.

Youniss, J. & Smollar, J. (1985). <u>Adolescent Relations With Mothers, Fathers and Friends</u>. University of Chicago Press: Chicago, Illinois.

Zaleznik, A., deVrics, M.F.R. & Howard, J. (1977). Stress reactions in organization: Syndromes, causes and consequences. <u>Behavioral Science</u>, 22, 151-162.

NOTES

NOTES

NOTES

NOTES